☆

THE LIMITS
OF AMERICAN
CAPITALISM

☆

BOOKS BY ROBERT L. HEILBRONER

The Limits of American Capitalism
Understanding Macroeconomics
A Primer on Government Spending (with Peter L. Bernstein)
The Great Ascent
The Making of Economic Society
The Future as History
The Quest for Wealth
The Worldly Philosophers

Robert L. Heilbroner

 THE LIMITS
OF AMERICAN
CAPITALISM

Harper & Row, Publishers
New York

FIRST EDITION

LIBRARY OF CONGRESS CATALOG CARD NUMBER: 66-21708
DESIGNED BY THE ETHEREDGES

☆

FOR W. H. FERRY

☆

☆

CONTENTS

☆

☆

PART I
CAPITALISM IN
AMERICA

☆

☆ 1 ☆

For roughly the past century and a half the dominant system of economic organization in most of the Western
world has been that of capitalism. In all likelihood, barring
the advent of a catastrophic war, capitalism will continue as
the dominant system of the Western world during the re-
mainder of this century and well into the next. The specter
of its overthrow by violent revolution has now receded
into the background. Capitalism will inevitably change,
may well suffer considerable duress over the next decades,
and in the longer run will gradually give way to a very

3

different kind of social order. But for our lives and for those of our children, it bids fair to confront us as the prevailing form of social organization in those nations where it is now solidly entrenched.

It seems to me that all serious social analysis and prediction in regard to the future of the West, and in particular of America, must start from some such premise. At any rate, it is my premise, and in this short book I propose to explore—with all the uncertainties and risks inherent in such an enterprise—the possibilities and impossibilities for American society implicit in such a view.

But at the outset a problem presents itself. Before we can speak of the possibilities that may be open to or closed off from America by virtue of its capitalist structure, we need to understand clearly what we mean by this structure. And that is by no means a simple matter. It is apparent, for example, that European capitalism or nineteenth- and twentieth-century capitalisms are all very different from the contemporary American kind: compare the worlds of Proust, Mann, Sinclair Lewis, and J. P. Marquand. Such reflections warn us against the dangers of treating the problem on too large and abstract a scale, and advise us to narrow our attention to the one historic and national manifestation of capitalism that most concerns us—capitalism in America today.

Yet this still fails to answer the question of what we mean by capitalism. For within contemporary America, how much of the society as a whole does that term include?

How much of the institutional framework, how much of national policy, how much of "life" do we describe when we call America a "capitalist" nation?

The question in this form remains very difficult to answer. But if we change our terminology ever so slightly, the problem suddenly becomes simpler. Instead of asking, "What are the boundaries of capitalism?" let us ask, "What are the boundaries of the business system?" For once we focus on the familiar institutions of the business world rather than on the shadowy elements of capitalism, the task of circumscribing the economic system and its penetration into the social environment becomes much more empirically meaningful. It is a great deal easier to talk about the place of business in society than the place of capitalism within society. Yet we are saying much the same thing. Capitalism and business are, after all, virtually synonymous—*capitalism* being the historian's term for the system abstractly conceived, *business* the common word for the system in its daily operation.

Moreover, once we substitute the institutions of business for those of capitalism, an important element of the problem quickly comes to the fore. It is that business, no matter how central to those societies we designate as "capitalist," is obviously not the only social structure around which those societies are built. The institutions of government, of course, long antedate the modern business firm, as do the universities and the churches and the military establishments. Even business itself, in the very different form of the guild and the state workshop, predates business as we know it today, and the earlier incarnations have lingered on in numerous ways to shape and constrain the later manifestation.

Hence the business world which is so much the active center of things in capitalist societies has always had to recognize the existence of other spheres of power and centers of influence, and to reconcile itself to areas of life in which its sway was disputed or even overruled by older— and in some ways more "legitimate"—sources of authority. What is more, this division of influence within capitalist society, as between the hegemony of the business and non-business worlds, has itself continually altered. Indeed, the history of capitalism can be conceived in large part as a continuing struggle to find an acceptable balance between the hyperactive business sector that is the dynamo of the system and the sometimes more passive, but still indispensable, nonbusiness structures that shape and define life outside the economic realm.

It is not difficult, I think, to describe the outcome of that struggle over the first century and a half of capitalism— roughly, let us say, from the early Industrial Revolution until the climactic period before the Great Depression. These were the years when the business world swelled within the social and political and cultural spheres of society, steadily dominating more and more activity in all fields. We can trace this continuous expansion of the presence of business in many ways. One is the rise of enormous enterprises as the focal points for the oganization of economic life. Another is the emergence of an economic ideology rivaling in importance that of the political, and far surpassing in practical significance that of the religious, creeds. Still a third is the relative decline in prestige and importance of such precapitalist groups as the nobility, the clergy, the military, and even the statesman. A fourth is the gradual rise of business ambitions and business anxieties as the predominant concerns of men and women throughout the Western world.

Nowhere was this process of business enlargement more clearly visible than in the United States. To compare the sheer economic weight of business enterprises within the national economy in 1800, 1850, 1900, and 1929, or the quantity and insistence of business propaganda over these years; or to appraise the general esteem accorded the churchman, the schoolteacher, or the governing official, compared with the entrepreneur; or simply to reconstruct the content of the table talk of America over these decades, is to present a succession of scenes in which the enormous magnification of business in relation to every other aspect of society is the most unmistakable single feature.

I do not think that many will quarrel with the assertion that the years before the onset of the Great Depression were marked by a steady and powerful expansion of business power and importance within American society. It is the years since then that are puzzling. On the one hand,

we have the development of truly gigantic business enterprises, an unparalleled proliferation of business propaganda,
and an unprecedentedly widespread acceptance of the
business system among the public at large. On the other
hand, there is the plain fact that business no longer occupies
quite the same position in regard to other centers of influence that it did only a generation ago. Thus we have the
paradoxical situation in which business seems to have extended still further its penetration into society at large,
while at the same time it appears more hedged about and
constricted than formerly. If this impression is correct it
would follow that capitalism itself must be in a state of
dynamic tension, at once more solidly entrenched and yet
more insecure than in the past. Let us look further into the
situation of business to see if this is so.

☆ 2 ☆

The place to begin an appraisal of the position of business within American society is with an examination of the
business terrain itself. For prior to tracing the ramifications
of a business "presence" throughout society, we must first
have a clear picture of the structure of business as it exists
at present.

There are in the United States today some eleven to
twelve million business "enterprises," counting the smallest

newsstand and the largest corporation as one enterprise each. This enormous multitude of proprietorships, partnerships, and corporations is of the greatest importance when we seek to describe the texture of American capitalism. Here is the source of its innumerable shops and stalls and lettered windows, of the voluminous yellow pages of its phone books, and not least, of the pervasive middle-class air of its politics—it has been estimated that the astonishing proportion of one fifth to almost a third of all urban workers have at one time or another—however briefly and insecurely—been "in business" for themselves.

Yet, as everyone knows, to identify these twelve million enterprises does not accurately describe the economic terrain, because it fails to locate the center of gravity within the American business world. For this we must look to the few giant enterprises whose economic weight vastly overbalances the multitudes of smaller enterprises. Thus the largest single enterprise in America, the American Telephone and Telegraph Company, all by itself accounts for almost 5 percent of the entire nonbanking corporate assets in the country. If we were to make the generous assumption that the average individual enterprise had assets of $25,000, A.T.&T. would balance evenly in the scales against one million smaller enterprises.

Between the extremes of the microscopic units of the economy—the roughly ten million small farms, stores, service businesses, and personal ventures that make up so much of the visible façade of American capitalism—and the towering monolith of A.T.&T. lies the bulk of the business units that carry on the main economic work of the nation. The million or so companies, largely corporations, that lie above the one-man business level do roughly five times the business of the ten million proprietorships.

Most of these corporations in turn, however, are small. Well over half of them do less than $100,000 a year in sales, with the result that this half, in total, accounts for only 2 percent of the business of the corporations as a whole. This leaves us with approximately half a million corporations who do 98 percent of the corporate business—which means that they do about three out of every four dollars' worth of all business, corporate or not, in the country. But here too, although the small firms outnumber the large, the large overshadow the small. One tenth of one percent of the bigger industrial corporations—a mere 500 firms at the top of the list—account by themselves for about one third of all the activity in the corporate industrial field.

Most studies of the concentration of business size focus on the preponderance of these top 500 manufacturing companies. Yet in many ways this still casts the net too wide. For one thing it obscures the concentration of strength *within* the concentrate itself, causing us to lose sight of the fact that the top 50 industrials enjoy an aggregate of sales as large as that of the bottom 450, and that the profits of the top *ten* companies are equal to almost half those of the remaining 490. And then, too, the bottom corporations on a list of 500 are not very impressive, as big businesses go. The 500th firm on the *Fortune* magazine list for 1964, for example, is the Draper Corporation, which had *sales* of only $97 million—less than the *profits* earned by twenty-six out of the fifty biggest firms.

Hence for the purposes of demonstrating the commanding position of the biggest businesses in the American economy, let us cross over the boundary lines of industrial companies into the world of finance, transportation, power, and retail sales, and assemble a roster of companies whose only qualification will be the ownership of a billion dollars' worth of assets or the sales of a billion dollars' worth of goods or services. This will give us roughly the top fifty industrial firms, the top forty banks, the top twenty insurance companies, the top ten merchandisers, the top ten transportation companies, and the top twenty utilities—150 companies in all.

How big are these 150 companies within the American economy? No single measure can give us an answer. Let us instead imagine that some curiously selective catastrophe obliterated just these 150 firms from the ranks of the twelve million American enterprises. What would disappear with them?

To begin with, the nation would come to a standstill. Not only would the Union and the Southern Pacific, the Pennsylvania, the New York Central, and a half dozen of the other main railroads of the nation vanish, leaving the cities to starve, but the possibilities of supplying the urban population by truck would also disappear as the main gasoline companies and the tire companies—not to mention the makers of cars and trucks—would also cease to exist. Meanwhile, within the nine largest concentrations of urban population all activity would have stopped with the termination of light and power, as the utilities in these areas vanished. In addition, communication in all areas would break down with the disappearance of the telephone company.

If we make the heroic assumption that the cities would survive, the problem would be to reconstitute the productive capacity of the remaining firms. This would have to be done without the steel capacity of the United States, Bethlehem, and Republic steel companies, the chemical output of Du Pont, Monsanto, Union Carbide, and Dow Chemical, the electrical machinery of General Electric and Westinghouse, or the transportation equipment made by Caterpillar Tractor, General Motors, and Ford. Meanwhile the farm sector would have to readjust to the disappearance of the agricultural machinery of International Harvester, the processing equipment of Swift, Armour, General Foods, Proctor and Gamble, National Dairy, and Bordens, and the indispensable containers provided by the big can companies.

Distribution patterns would have collapsed with the disappearance of the A.&P., First National, Safeway, Food Fair, Krogers, Penney, Woolworth, Sears, and Montgomery Ward. Defense would have crumbled with the removal of General Electric, I.B.M., Sperry Rand, and the makers of virtually all planes and missiles. A national credit debacle would have followed the closing of the Chase Manhattan, First National, Bankers Trust, Manufacturers Hanover, Chemical, Morgan Guaranty, and Irving Trust banks in New York, and their counterparts in San Francisco, Chicago, Los Angeles, Pittsburgh, Detroit, Boston, Cleveland, Philadelphia, Dallas, Seattle, Portland, and Milwaukee, not to mention Buffalo, Winston-Salem, Mineola, and Houston. With these top forty banks would also go the twenty biggest insurance companies, taking with them $500 billion in life insurance, and effectively bankrupting a majority of American families.

We need not press the point further. It is clear that the removal of 150 supercorporations would effectively destroy the American economy—a catastrophe that must be compared with the near-equanimity with which we face the regular disappearance of a hundred times that many businesses due to the bankruptcies that annually thin the ranks of the business world at large.

To be sure, we should beware against assuming that the arbitrary measure of $1 billion automatically selects the most important corporations in America. It includes some companies, like the railroads that are big but weak, and excludes others, like the nonferrous metals group, that are smaller but strategically important. It makes no distinction between companies that are declining in importance and those that are rising. Not least, it excludes all but one of the important centers for the manufacture of opinion—

the National Broadcasting Company (a subsidiary of R.C.A.) is among the top 150 supercorporations, but not Time, Inc. (which nevertheless ranks 146th on the list of the industrial giants), or the *New York Times* or Chicago *Tribune*, neither of which appears at all.

Nonetheless, with all its oversimplifications and inaccuracies, the list of the supercorporations makes one point clear beyond cavil. It is that a tiny group of immense corporations constitutes a bastion of formidable economic strength within the sprawling expanse of the American economy—indeed, that it forms a virtual economic system within an economic system. Our appraisal of the position of business within American society must begin with that cardinal fact.

That big business dominates the economic landscape will hardly come as much of a surprise to most readers, although the extent of the concentration of economic power is always something of a shock. What is important, however, is not the mere existence of concentration in itself, but the consequences of that central fact. Hence we must now turn from an essentially static description of the place of giant business within the economy to the more demanding task of describing the dynamic operation of these huge units on the economic scene.

The first question that begs our attention is one that emerges directly from the statistics we have just examined. Are the giant corporations continuing to grow still larger within the business scene? Can we expect the degree of concentration to increase still further in the future?

In 1932 when Adolf A. Berle and Gardiner Means published a pioneering statistical and conceptual study of this question, the evidence showed that concentration *was* increasing, and at an alarming rate. Between 1909 and 1929, the 200 largest nonfinancial corporations had increased their ownership of assets 40 percent faster than the rest of business. Berle and Means made the half-fanciful calculation that if these big companies continued to grow at this rate, in due course all business would be fused into one gigantic corporation with a life expectancy equal to that of the Roman Empire. That fearful date was still some 360 years in the future, but long before that—by 1950, in fact —Berle and Means warned that a continuation of the observed growth of concentration would give the two hundred largest nonfinancial corporations the ownership of 70 percent of all nonfinancial corporate wealth.

Berle and Means's target date is now some fifteen years behind us, so that we should be able to check on the accuracy of their forebodings. Certainly there is evidence that the broad trend of their studies continues. The large corporation has continued to grow, in terms of total assets, faster than its smaller brethren, so that, for example, whereas the top 100 industrial corporations owned 25 percent of all industrial corporate wealth in 1929, they owned 31 percent in 1960. Similarly, the measurement of their total displacement, when calculated on the basis of "value added" in manufacturing, shows a rise from 23 percent in 1947 to 30 percent in 1958.

Impressive as these rates of growth are, they are a good deal less than those implicit in Berle and Means's figures. Moreover, although the large corporation continues to loom larger each year over the corporate or industrial sector of the nation, it is not clear that it looms larger over the entire economy. Due to the very rapid growth of the service sector, the proportion of national income originating in the corporate sector—a proportion that has grown steadily since the development of the corporation—has recently begun to decline. According to Victor Fuchs, apparently a peak was reached in 1955 when corporations accounted for 55.8 percent of national income. By 1963 this had receded to 53.8 percent, approximately the level of 1948.

Thus it would seem that the headlong momentum of the big corporations within the total economy was no longer that of the 1920's. Perhaps equally important, there is considerable evidence that their displacement within their respective industrial fields is no longer significantly rising. According to the calculations of M. A. Adelman of M.I.T., the level of concentration within industrial markets has slowed down to "the pace of a glacial drift." With a few exceptions, such as the automobile industry, we find the percentage of business accruing to the biggest firms in different industrial fields to be more or less stationary. That is, for each industry in which we can detect a drift toward the increased predominance of the largest firms, there seems to be another in which the opposite is true. A small sampling of the fifty largest industries shows us this:

PERCENTAGE OF SHIPMENTS MADE BY
LARGEST FOUR COMPANIES IN SPECIFIED INDUSTRIES

	1947	1958
Motor vehicles and parts	56	75
Blast furnaces and steel mills	50	53
Petroleum refining	37	32
Meat packing	41	34
Radios and related parts	26	27
Tires and tubes	77	74
Beer and ale	21	28
Plastics materials	44	40
Tin cans	78	80
Tractors	67	69
Bottled soft drinks	10	11
Synthetic fibers	78	78
Motors and generators	59	47

SOURCE: *U.S. Statistical Abstract, 1965, pp. 788–790.*

Sadly, we do not have figures that would allow us to make similar comparisons for banks, insurance or transportation companies, merchandisers, or utilities. There seems no doubt, however, that in at least one of these fields—utilities—the degree of concentration since the late 1920's and early 1930's must have decreased substantially due to the breakup of the utility holding companies. Contrariwise, it is likely that banking concentration has increased, due to the considerable number of mergers among large banks during the late 1940's and 1950's, and it is also likely that the growth of the big merchandising firms has taken a larger share of the retail market than in 1929. On the other hand, this concentrative trend is by no means the rule with the transportation market.

In short, the conclusion seems to be that the ballooning of the biggest corporations within the industrial sector, although continuing, has been taking place at a much reduced pace from that of the era of the late 1920's, and that the domination of the biggest firms within their own industries seems to have largely stabilized. This has, needless to say, very important consequences. If the power of big business rests, at least in part, on the sheer bulk of the large corporation within the economy, the evidence tells us that this base of power has lost some of its erstwhile expansionary thrust. At worst, the giant corporation continues slowly to expand within the borders of the business world as a whole; at best, it seems to be "contained" within the smaller subworlds of its industrial markets. In either event, the once imminently threatening engulfment of business by the giant corporation no longer seems likely to occur.

But why has the rate of growth of the industrial giants slowed down at all?

Curiously, the reasons are not wholly clear. One commonly offered explanation, for example, attributes the slowdown to the impact of strengthened antitrust legislation and tougher antitrust enforcement policies on the expansion plans of the biggest firms. In a number of important instances, some of which we shall encounter later, antitrust has broken a large company into smaller components, and in a few cases impending mergers that would have significantly increased the degree of concentration—such as the proposed Bethlehem-Youngstown Steel merger—have been prevented by government action.

Yet at best the force of antitrust can only have been a partial factor in preventing or inhibiting growth. For one thing, the merger trend has been steadily rising since the 1940's, although it is not quite back to the level of the late 1920's. For another, from 1951 to 1961 the fifty largest industrial firms swallowed 471 firms without government demurrer. Even more to the point, it is uncertain that mergers constitute a major avenue for corporate growth. According to a study of seventy-four large firms by J. Fred Weston, mergers were responsible for no more than one-quarter of their expansion, and thus the government's antimerger policy would explain at best only a small part of the observed slowdown in the growth of the biggest companies.

A second explanation for the failure of the largest companies to continue their earlier rates of expansion stresses the winnowing force of changing patterns of economic demand. There is no question that some such mechanism explains the failure of many great corporations of an earlier day to retain their one-time rank among the largest companies. Looking at the list of the fifty largest industrial concerns in 1909 we note among the casualties the Central Leather Company, then the seventh largest company in the nation, the victim of plastic poisoning; the decline of the

Pullman Company from eighth in rank in 1909 to 124th in 1964, undercut by the encroachment of new modes of transportation which it was powerless to affect; the disappearance (by absorption into another company) of the American Locomotive Company as its main product became obsolete; the fall of American Woolen before the onslaughts of synthetic textiles. If we looked at the nonindustrial firms we would also find the movie companies, among the largest enterprises in 1929, relegated to secondary roles in 1964 by the incursion of television, as well as by an antitrust divorcement from the theater business.

Conversely, if we look at the top fifty firms for 1964 we find that most of them have risen to giant size by catering to currents of demand that the previous incumbents failed to satisfy. At least thirteen of the present biggest industrial companies have appeared simply by virtue of the rise of automobile transportation with its related rubber and petroleum industries—helped again by the famous antitrust finding against Standard Oil that split one immense firm into a number of fragments, four of which have grown big enough in themselves to make the list of the top fifty. Other beneficiaries of rising demand for special products are I.B.M., Western Electric (manufacturer for A.T.&T.), or Radio Corporation of America—not to mention at least five companies that have made the list solely because of defense and space expenditures. In all, of the fifty biggest firms in 1964 thirty-three did not appear among the top fifty in 1909, and virtually every one of these owes its rise to its ability to have created a new product or satisfied a new demand.

Yet the forces of technology and changing patterns of demand do not explain why the pace of industrial concentration has slowed down since the beginning of the 1940's. After all, technology and demand helped and hindered the growth of firms in earlier years just as they do today; indeed, it is likely that the displacing effect of both was greater in the earlier years of the century than it is now. For despite the slowdown in the growth of the biggest companies, if we trace the roster of big firms from 1909 to the present, we find that the rate of dropout falls. Between 1909 and 1919, for example, nineteen of the top fifty industrial companies gave way to other firms. Between 1948 and 1960—a slightly longer period of time—only fourteen firms were shouldered aside. Between 1960 and 1964 but four have dropped. It would seem, then, that the difficulty of ousting the biggest firms is growing, a fact that would argue against the emergence of new firms as the main factor in bringing about a halt in the domination by the biggest.

What is the reason, then, for the unmistakable slowing down of the supercorporations? There seems to be no single decisive explanation. One contributory factor is certainly the unfriendly attitude of the government toward any corporate expansion that would seriously change the texture of certain critical markets. For example, General Motors in 1964 made four times as much profit as the entire assets of American Motors, and by cutting its prices for a year or two could unquestionably drive its rival out of the field, perhaps along with Chrysler as well. But such behavior, which might have been acceptable in the mid-nineteenth century—it was the standard tactic of the railroads in their struggles for individual supremacy—would be "unthinkable" today, largely for fear of risking government suit.

A second reason for the slowdown no doubt lies in the prosperous state of the economy since 1940. Professor Adelman, although finding no tendency to greater concentration today, believes that it increased during the depression years, when the weaker firms went under, and warns that another depression might well result in another surge of corporate amalgamation.

Third, many of the largest companies have reached a more or less stable balance of power within their own fields and now seek expansion by diversifying in other fields. This accounts for their growing "global" bulk, but at the same time their diversification exposes them to competition in new markets, in many of which they must contend with smaller but more specialized and well-entrenched companies. A study by A. D. H. Kaplan shows that in a thousand different product "classes" or markets the 100 biggest firms are not even among the biggest four sellers in almost half the markets, that they are only one out of the four biggest sellers in another 231 markets, and that they themselves constitute the biggest four sellers in only thirty-three cases. Thus the very diversity that protects the over-all economic security of the supercorporation may militate against the rapid expansion characteristic of the time when it was a more specialized concern.

All these reasons help explain the phenomenon of economic slowdown among the biggest firms. There remains, however, a final reason that must not be omitted from our analysis. This is the possibility that big business is no longer expanding as rapidly as in the halcyon days of the early twentieth century because it is no longer being run by a group of executives who are as unabashedly aggressive as were the founding fathers and early corporate managers of these companies. The possibility exists, in other words, that at least one factor making for the "containment" of big business is the replacement of a generation of acquisitors by one of administrators, interested of course in growth, but more concerned with the long-run survival and stability of their firms than with the single-minded aim of making them as big as they possibly can in their traditional areas of business.

☆ 3 ☆

This suggestion leads us away from the measurable to the immeasurable aspects of the position of business within the economy. In particular, it turns our attention from the more or less quantifiable dimensions of the marketplace to the intangible questions of the attitudes and outlooks of the men who wield the power in the biggest companies.

What sort of men run the American supercorporation? What are their goals, their values? Fifty or sixty years ago it would have been much easier to form an opinion about the views and motivations of the business elite, for the supercorporations of those days were still largely dominated by the supermen who started them. Not alone the names but the personalities of Rockefeller, Morgan, Harriman, Carnegie, Ford, and Frick were familiar to everyone. Even though these baronial figures were by no means wholly representative of the already fast bureaucratizing business structure, their "style" of leadership—aggressive, colorful, intensely personal—made the nature and exercise of big business power both vivid and intuitively comprehensible. The same was still true thirty-five years ago when the supermen had already almost disappeared from view, and the reins of power were held by a few centers of finance capital. Although marked by less clear-cut personalities than the original generation of entrepreneurial acquisitors, the great investment banking houses of Morgan Stanley, Kuhn Loeb, National City—in short, Wall Street —at least constituted a clearly demarcated social group in which to locate and examine business leadership.

Today it is not so simple to identify or dissect the business elite, for Wall Street too has receded into the mists. We are left with a largely faceless group known as "management." How many well-informed people, for example, can name even one of the chief executive officers—with the exception of Henry Ford, Jr.—of the top ten industrial companies: General Motors, Standard Oil (N.J.), Ford, General Electric, Socony, U.S. Steel, Chrysler, Texaco, Gulf, Western Electric? How many can name the top figures in the ten top utilities or banks—perhaps with the exception of David Rockefeller?

This anonymity of management does not mean that power in the supercorporations can no longer be located within the hands of a relatively few identifiable men. The word "management" blurs over critical distinctions among the officialdom of business, clothing in an identical gray flannel both the salaried help, whose independent decision-making authority is often very much less than their vice-presidential titles or very substantial salaries would indicate, and a small inner group of genuinely top managers, whose authority and independence are very great. Even within the latter it may be necessary to distinguish between the "career" manager, be he president or even chairman of the board, whose day-to-day authority is unquestionably supreme, and the ultimate strategic power that lies with the largest financial owners of the great corporations. According to the careful estimates of Don Villarejo, in 141 out of 232 largest industrials there are identifiable ownership interests of at least 5 percent of the shares, and Gabriel Kolko calculates that in the top 100 industrial corporations, directors owned or controlled at least 10 percent of the *voting* stock, although in many cases their ownership of all stock reduced their visible interest in the corporation far below that figure. Thus there remains a small group of very powerful financial interests mingled with the somewhat larger group of operational top managers. Among the 150 supercorporations, there are perhaps as many as 1,500 or 2,000 operational top managers, but as few as 200 to 300 families own blocks of stock that ultimately control these corporations.

To what degree do these richest families or groups *use* their voting power to influence the operations of "their" companies? We do not know. There exists a shroud of secrecy over the relation between the centers of inherited wealth and the determination of working policy in capitalism. It is likely, however, that this secrecy testifies more to the nature of the shibboleths and values of the business system than to anything particularly sinister or even significant in the use of that power. It is certain that the centers of voting power have an important voice in the initial selection of the working management, but it is also probable that if that management proves itself to be competent, the financial centers are content with a passive role.

Thus our inquiry into the attitude and outlook of big business leads us to ask who is the working management. Two contrary myths are generally in circulation about it. According to one, the men at the top are those who have risen there from humble circumstances by virtue of their superior abilities and stubborn efforts. This myth has been considerably abetted by businessmen themselves who like to exaggerate the steepness of the climb behind them. The *Scientific American* magazine in 1964 undertook a survey of the background characteristics of the 1,000 top executives—generally presidents and chairmen—of 600 leading industrial corporations who filled out questionnaires about their careers. Almost a quarter claimed to come from "poor" families, and only 10 percent rated their families as "wealthy." Dr. Mabel Newcomer, surveying a substantially similar group fifteen years earlier, but investigating family circumstances independently, found the percentage of "poor" families to be only half as large and that of "wealthy" families to be three times as great.

On the other hand, it is not an ingrown elite, which effectively spikes a second myth—that the top executives are mainly the sons of top executives. On the contrary, in 1964, again according to the *Scientific American* survey, only 6 percent of the top corporate officials were sons of heads of the same companies. More striking, less than half (43 percent) of the whole group of top executives had fathers who were independent businessmen. The majority (51 percent) came from "middle-class" employee or professional families.

Not only their socioeconomic backgrounds but also their career patterns are inconspicuous. Less than 3 percent of the corporate elite today describes its principal occupational experience as that of "entrepreneur" or "capitalist," and most executives trace their rise through administration or science and engineering. By way of contrast, as recently as 1925, almost a third of the then top executives were "entrepreneurs" or "capitalists," and in 1900 half were. As a result of this decline in business-building, formal education has achieved a much greater significance in paving the way for corporate leadership. As recently as the 1920's a majority of top corporate officials did not have a college degree. Today nearly 90 percent have been to college, three-quarters have a B.A. or B.S., and a third hold graduate degrees, increasingly in engineering or science.

Thus there has been an unmistakable bureaucratization among the topmost managerial echelons—a shift from the self-made, self-serving tycoon to the company-made, company-serving "manager." The late Paul Baran summed up the contrast this way:

> There are many ways to describe the contrast between the tycoon and modern manager. The former was the parent of the giant corporation, the latter is its child. The tycoon stood outside and above, dominating the corporation. The manager is an insider, dominated by it. The loyalty of the one was to himself and his family . . . the loyalty of the other is to the organization to which he belongs and through which he expresses himself. To one the corporation was merely a means to enrichment; to the other the good of the company has become both an economic and ethical end. The one stole from the company, the other steals for it.

This brief survey of the background of big business management adds confirmation to the suggestion that part of the decline in the growth rate of big business can be traced to subtle and pervasive changes in the aims and attitudes of its controlling management. There remains the question, however, of how the present management views its wider role, of what its social as well as economic aims and goals may be and of how it sees the relationship between its own world of business and the rest of society. In short, our investigation into the position of business within American society brings us to the crucial consideration of the ideology of the corporate elite.

Ideologies always yield penetrating insights into the attitudes of dominant classes, but it is not easy in a business society, where ideology has no official font, to know exactly what statements can be taken "seriously" as representing the way business feels about things. Often we feel we learn more from a chance remark—Charles Wilson's famous statement that "What is good for General Motors is good for the United States and vice versa"—than from the studied "position papers" of the National Association of Manufacturers or the Chamber of Commerce. But, while such remarks give an intense brief flash of light, they fail to illumine the whole terrain of business opinion in a systematic way. Hence a number of efforts have been made to study the "official" positions of organizations such as the N.A.M., or the Committee for Economic Development, a much more liberal-minded business study group. The trouble, however, is that many firms belong both to the N.A.M. and to the C.E.D., and thereby implicitly endorse policies that are often considerably at variance with one another.

Fortunately, a much more apposite source exists for our purposes in a series of lectures delivered annually since 1956 under the auspices of the McKinsey Foundation at the Graduate School of Business of Columbia University. The purpose of the lectures, in the words of the first speaker, Ralph Cordiner, Chairman of General Electric, was "to coax us businessmen out of our offices and into the arena of public thought where our managerial philosophies can be put to the test of examination by men trained in other disciplines." The fact that Cordiner was succeeded by the late T. V. Houser, Chairman of Sears Roebuck, Crawford Greenewalt, President of Du Pont, Roger Blough, Chairman of U.S. Steel, Frederick Kappel, President of A.T.&T., and Thomas Watson, Chairman of I.B.M., testifies to the willingness of the highest corporate elite to respond to that challenge.

There can be little doubt that the McKinsey lectures constitute a serious effort to define the "managerial philosophy" of the respective lecturers. As we would expect, the speeches vary considerably from speaker to speaker, in style as well as substance. Yet when we read them in their entirety, threads of common concern begin to detach themselves from the variety of the texts. Let us try to present those common elements as succinctly as possible.

One thing immediately strikes a reader of these essays. It

is something about the tone of discourse that emerges from the very initial paragraph in Cordiner's opening address:

> *Many thoughtful persons have observed that the United States has evolved a wholly new form of capitalism, variously called democratic capitalism, mass capitalism, or—more aptly—people's capitalism. As the first nation in the world to break through the ancient barriers of scarcity into a world of abundance, we have a unique experience that we ourselves need fully to understand and to communicate to the rest of the world. But somehow we have not been able to do it well—to describe this new people's capitalism, and all that it means to the spiritual and cultural life of the people, as well as to their material well-being.*

It is a curiously reflective, diffident, and even plaintive statement, and one that contrasts sharply with the assertive tone of business pronouncements of another age. But this cautious tone—discernible throughout nearly all the lectures—is not the only identifying thread among the various speakers. Of greater interest are a series of substantive statements about the nature of big business and its relationship to the rest of society which occur with surprising consistency from one lecture to the next.

The first of those we have already seen in Cordiner's statement. It is the contention that contemporary American capitalism is "new," and therefore not to be charged with the sins of its predecessor. As T. V. Houser writes: "The historic complaint that big business, as the producing arm of capitalism, exploited the many for the profit of the few and deprived the workers of the products of their own labor had a valid basis in the facts of European capitalism, but lacks substance when applied to American capitalism today."

What are the hallmarks of this new capitalism? A number of themes emerge from the lectures. One is the universal recognition that big units of business rather than small individual enterprises are now the economic backbone of our industrial society. As Roger Blough puts it: "The American public has gradually become accustomed to larger and larger groups and has become convinced that big production groups are outstanding in reliability and in the quality of their products and services and are necessary to perform America's larger production tasks in research, in production, and in the procurement of raw materials." "Without large-scale economic enterprises," echoes Cordiner, "a nation is today a second-rate power."

Thus the new ideology is in part a rationale for the bigness of business. There is, however, a further recognition that goes along with the frank admission of the need for large-scale units in business. It is that businesses are now charged with special responsibilities, particularly with respect to the complex task of balancing the claims of their various constituencies—labor, stockholder, customer, supplier. "We all know that special power imposes special responsibilities on those who hold it," writes Thomas Watson. "Even if nothing else had changed, the vast concentrations of power in our society would demand that business-men reconsider their responsibilities for the broader public welfare." Cordiner repeats the gist: "The important principle I should like to suggest here, in relations with customers, share owners, employees, suppliers, educational institutions, charitable activities, government and the general public, is that all activities must be guided by the recognition of common purposes and of the contribution that each group makes toward their achievement."

How is this adjudicatory function to be fulfilled? The answer is that the big businessman is no longer just tied to narrow self-interest. Rather he has become—perhaps by virtue of his bureaucratic career line—a new kind of business executive: a *professional*. Note, for example, that Cordiner entitles his lecture *New Frontiers for Professional Managers*.

We shall have a chance shortly to consider the validity of this self-portrait. But first let us pay heed to a last and most important common element in the statements of the McKinsey lecturers. It is the more or less hesitant concession of a new legitimacy to the main centers of power that contest with business: labor and government. To be sure, the predominant attitude of the two most conservative McKinsey speakers, Blough and Cordiner, is one of distrust and misgiving: Blough speaks of the "glacier-like" power of labor unions, whose "strength and influence can hardly be overestimated," and we are alerted by Cordiner to "the fantastically growing federal government" with its untoward consequences for the business system. Yet even these two speakers are careful to preface their remarks with tributes to the propiety of labor organization and to the essential role played by government in sustaining the level of economic activity.

Much more striking is the view expressed by Thomas J. Watson of I.B.M.:

> *Much as we may dislike it, I think we've got to realize that in our kind of society there are times when government has to step in and help people with some of their more difficult problems. Programs which assist Americans by reducing the hazards of a free market system without damaging the system itself are necessary, I believe, to its survival. . . .*
>
> *To be sure, the rights and guarantees that the average man believes in and insists upon may interfere, to some degree, with our ability to manage our enterprises with complete freedom of action. As a result, there are businessmen who either ignore or deny these claims. They then justify their views by contending that if we were to recognize or grant them, the whole system of free enterprise would be endangered.*
>
> *This, it would seem to me, amounts to an open invitation to exactly the kind of government intervention that businessmen are seeking to avoid. For if we businessmen insist that free enterprise permits us to be indifferent to those things on which people put high value, then the people will quite naturally assume that free enterprise has too much freedom.*

All these quotations do not, of course, definitively formulate the ideology of big business. At best the McKinsey lectures gives us glimpses into the ideas that certain very important businessmen seek to present as their "managerial philosophy" to an academic but not unfriendly audience. Yet I believe it is possible to find sufficient confirmation of the general point of view of these lectures to enable us to attempt a few generalizations about the view held by big businessmen as to the role of business within society at large.

Let me begin with a few critical words. It must be apparent that a great deal of cant, of more or less conscious hypocrisy, accompanies the sober and seemingly enlightened expressions of the McKinsey lecturers. The stress on the "newness" of capitalism, for example, carefully avoids a recitation of those facts, such as the distribution of wealth or income, that testify to profound structural continuities rather than change; the "frank" confrontation of bigness in business does not extend to a public discussion of the concentration of business power; and the repeated stress on "professionalism" glosses over the fact that the meaning of the word when applied to business behavior is very far removed from any meaning it has in the nonbusiness world.

This last point is worth another word. The idea of a "professional manager" is certainly a highly appealing one, conjuring up the image of a corps of highly competent and dedicated men who will discharge with a fine disinterest the demanding tasks of running a complex organization. Thus *Fortune's* editors enthuse over the professional manager who has "a responsibility to society as a whole"; and even the *Scientific American,* in reviewing the fact of a growing

technical background for high executives, is led to conclude that this is evidence of a trend to "professionalism."

Unfortunately it is not so easy to give substance to the
image. For one thing, the sanctions that play so important a
role in other professions are missing in business. The malpractitioner of law or medicine is disbarred by his own
colleagues from the further practice of his calling, but no
such punishment faces the malpractitioner of management.
For example, of the fifteen executives discharged by General Electric after being found guilty by the courts in the
electrical price-rigging case, twelve were subsequently re-
employed at high levels elsewhere. One was made president
of one of the companies surveyed by the *Scientific American*.

Then, too, it is hard to square the notion of professionalism with some of the attitudes and activities of top management in the postwar decades. Here one thinks of the
ignorance or complicity of the top executives in the electrical industry scandal; of the breach of faith shown President Kennedy by the steel companies in raising their prices;
of the indifference, not to say contempt, toward public
health displayed by the tobacco industry; of the lobbying
tactics of the drug companies during the Kefauver investigation into their pricing practices; of the omniscient denial
by the auto industry of the public's interest in compact cars
or safety belts; of the shameless loading of profits by the
biggest defense contractors (Western Electric, for example, made 31 percent on its Nike production; Douglas

Aircraft made 44 percent on its defense contracts); and not least of the arrogation to themselves by the "professional managers" of remunerations that in any other sphere of social activity—science, education, government—would be called piratical.*

These blatant discrepancies between preachment and reality tempt one to dismiss the entire declaration of the McKinsey lecturers as nothing more than a smoke screen, a camouflage behind which the old practices and beliefs may be more artfully concealed. Yet I think that such a dismissal would seriously misinterpret the meaning of the new ideology. For there is considerable evidence that a search for a more realistic "philosophy" for big business genuinely occupies the more thoughtful members of the business elite. We see this not alone in the content of numerous speeches but in the proliferation of executive training courses within large companies where top (or very near top) management

---

* For 1964 the take of the top men of the top ten corporations was as follows: Frederick Donner, Chairman, General Motors, $200,400 salary plus $453,750 bonus; M. J. Rathbone, Chairman, Standard Oil of New Jersey, $300,000 salary plus $135,000 bonus plus $24,652 credited to Thrift Plan; Henry Ford II, Chairman, Ford Motor Company, $200,000 salary plus $340,000 bonus; Fred J. Borch, President, General Electric, $237,534 salary plus 1,026 shares of stock at $85.25 a share; Albert A. Nickerson, Chairman, Cocony Mobil Oil, $200,000 salary plus $10,000 contribution to saving plan; Lynn A. Townsend, President, Chrysler Corporation, $179,200 salary plus incentive compensation of $376,700 payable over five years; Roger Blough, Chairman, United States Steel, $285,000 plus $11,400 contribution to savings fund; Augustus C. Long, Chairman, Texaco, $343,817 plus $7,488 paid to savings plan; Thomas J. Watson, Chairman, I.B.M., $100,000 plus $249,053 bonus; W. K. Whiteford, Chairman, Gulf Oil, $225,000 salary plus $175,020 incentive compensation payable over five years.

is deliberately exposed to critical opinion—not, needless to say, in the expectation that its executives will experience a crisis of faith, but rather to find "business answers" to criticisms of the business system. Then, again, the rise of the Committee for Economic Development, with its much more liberal tendencies than the National Association of Manufacturers or the Chamber of Commerce, or the unusual recruitment of business support for President Johnson's domestic policies and the relative absence of business support for Goldwater, all bespeak a recognition on the part of business of a changed environment, and an attempt, however limited or hypocritical, to explain and justify their role in it.

But just as we must refrain from dismissing as mere window dressing the ideological reformulations represented by the McKinsey lectures, so we must guard against the assumption that big business has now shifted en masse to a more liberal orientation. It would be more accurate, I think to stress the existence of a considerably wide spectrum of business opinion and to balance the views of the "new" management with those of an older vintage. In particular, there remains a right wing of business thought, represented by such figures as H. L. Hunt, the oil king who has long financed ultraconservative causes, or J. Howard Pew, Chairman of the Sun Oil Company (forty-seventh largest corporation in assets), who has been reported by the *Times* as giving $1 million to the Christian Freedom Foundation which calls urban renewal "Marxism" and which proposes that Communist nations be "driven" from the UN, or perhaps most significantly by Ralph Cordiner, who following his retirement from General Electric was prominently associated with the Goldwater movement.

Yet the existence of a vehement reactionary element among the leadership of the supercorporations should not be viewed out of proportion. After all, the big corporations donate many times more money than they give to right-wing groups to the universities and colleges where the prevailing view is certainly to the left of average business opinion. And, beyond that, it is unlikely that typical opinion among the big business elite is accurately represented by the outlook of the far Right. The fervid political commitment of the ultraconservative is not congenial to most big businessmen, who, like most Americans, are not fundamentally ideological creatures. Oratory and table thumping to the contrary notwithstanding, I think that what is noticeable among the majority of big businessmen in America is a striking absence of real political commitment. What is visible instead is a profound unwillingness to get embroiled in anything that might take them away from their jobs, or that might not look good in the newspapers, or that might displease their main customers or their boards.

Hence the natural attraction of big businessmen to the comfortable center of opinion, with its conservative, but not shockingly conservative, views. And thus all the more important that the tenets of this central opinion have departed so discernibly from the fundamentalism of a genera-

tion ago. In the concept of a "new" capitalism, character-
ized by large-scale units, searching for a "professional"
image for its managers, and aware—if only grudgingly—of
the legitimacy of labor and government as centers of economic power, we have an expression of what capitalism
means to the big business elite of the 1960's that is markedly different from what a corresponding declaration of
principles would have revealed in the 1920's or 1930's.

More important yet, the views of a Thomas Watson or a
T. V. Houser reveal that "center" opinion is flanked on the
left as well as on the right, and that a markedly more liberal
ideology may be in the process of formation. A very great
distance separates the views of a Blough or a Cordiner and
that of, for instance, Watson, who writes:

> My own company became involved with the Antitrust
> Division in 1952 and we now operate under a consent
> decree. It never seemed to me that this action gave me
> grounds to criticize the government. In fact I have fre-
> quently stated that I believed the law was a force for good
> and I have no quarrel with the decision in relation to IBM.

Is business opinion as a whole moving in the direction of
this kind of enlightened formulation? We shall return to
the question at the end of this essay. In the meantime it
seems reasonable to conclude that, however slowly, in-
completely, and ungraciously, the big business directorate
is trying to make its peace with the realities of the twentieth century.

There remains, however, a last point. Whatever may be the changing content of the ideology of big business, what can we say as to the influence of this ideology on the nation at large? Because big business bulks large within the economic system, do its ideas also bulk large within the system of opinons of society at large?

It is well to approach the question cautiously. Plainly the ideology of the business elite is not the only determinant of business—much less national—thought. The beliefs of the small and middle-sized business communities are by no means necessarily those of big business. Represented by their Chambers of Commerce, participating in the middle-class culture of lodges, sales conventions, and lower-echelon community organizations, the lower and middle ranks of businessmen tend to be less sophisticated than the upper reaches of the business world, and on many issues less open to adjustment. Traditionally, opposition to such measures as minimum wage laws, public spending, unionism, business regulation, or economic planning—not to mention liberal social policies—finds its most vociferous advocates in the millions of small-scale enterprises quite as much as, and ofttimes more than, among big businessmen.

In like fashion, much of the ceaseless drumfire of anti-Communist propaganda, which has come to be such a powerful force for the direction and misdirection of American energies, can also be attributed only in part to the efforts of big business, although, as we have seen, it has its protagonists there. It is in the middle- and lower-class strata that these sentiments, in all their most elementary appeal, find their most solid entrenchment, and even the academic world is not free from the virus of demonistic thinking.

Thus it would be a gross oversimplification to attribute the pressures of conservative opinion entirely to the more or less deliberately articulated views of leading businessmen —not that the latter all agree, as we have seen. Furthermore, as evidenced by the fruitless attempt of both big and little business to win support for the policies of the Republican party, even the combined efforts of businessmen of all kinds may be of little use in changing the political orientation of the public.

Business is, in other words, only one of several sources of public opinion, and big business is only one of several business sources. Nonetheless, that does not quite dispose of the matter. Big business may be unable to win support for specific policies or candidates, but it cannot be absolved from an important share of responsibility for the basic economic and social opinions of society.

Were the big business elite tomorrow to change its ideas and to endorse measures of social and economic reform with all the editorial and other influence that it possesses, I think few would deny that the political center of the country would probably move sharply and quickly to the left. To put it differently, one function of an existing ideology is to draw the lines for what is discussable and what is not, for what kinds of ideas are to be taken seriously and what kinds simply laughed out of court. It is often said that the people get what they want, but that statement is rarely followed by the question, "Why do they want what they want?"

We shall return at the very end of our essay to the crucial problem of the role of the business ideology in setting these general limits of opinion in America. Suffice it to suggest at this point that were the main instruments for the "enlightment" of the people not dominated by a general business orientation, and powerfully influenced by the views of big business, it seems very likely that the social and economic policies of this nation would be far more liberal than they are. To that extent the business ideology must bear a large measure of responsibility for the ideas that create and reinforce the status quo.

☆ 4 ☆

The elusive problem of the "power" of the business ideology leads us toward a problem that we have as yet failed to engage squarely. That is the over-all importance of big business in society today. What are the limits of its sway? Is its influence diminishing or increasing?

These questions plunge us still deeper into the seas of uncertainty and conjecture. But we can at least begin to discuss the problem objectively by focusing on one aspect that is fairly open to observation and empirical judgment. This is the oldest and purest exercise of economic power—the market exploitation of the weak.

Among those whom big business has exploited, the classic victim has been labor. For example, as late as 1919 the workweek at United States Steel consisted of a twelve-hour day and a seven-day week, with a 24-hour swing shift every other week—a schedule that was, according to Judge Gary and other steel officials, impossible to change. And then there is the familiar, if dreary, chronicle of the Ford assembly-line speedups and the Colorado Fuel and Iron company towns, of antiunion discrimination, yellow-dog contracts, and the like.

In point of fact, big business was never the only or the most culpable oppressor of labor. The most terrible sweatshops were in trades such as garment making where competition among numerous small entrepreneurs led to pitiless practices of cost cutting, or in agricultural fringe industries where poverty, fierce competition, and rural cruelty joined to create small hells of labor conditions. Yet throughout the late nineteenth and early twentieth centuries, the practices of big business toward its labor force—in the great mills, on the railroads, in the mass production factories—were harsh and indifferent at worst, patronizing at best.

Merely to call to mind this chapter of the past is to remind us that it has been written finis. Few would deny, I think, that the power relationship between big business and labor has been fundamentally changed, and that however fiercely labor may attack big business—and it is not very fiercely any more—it is not any longer afraid of the big corporation as it once was. Partly because of changes in labor legislation, itself testimony to a diminution of business influence, partly because of the greater ease, in today's market structure, in extracting more profit from a sales check than from a pay check, big business no longer exercises its market power over labor as in the past.

A second locus of big business power on the marketplace has been in regard to small business. We think, for instance, of Standard Oil who forced the railroads to charge its smaller competitors higher freight rates, the additional revenues from which were then turned over to Standard Oil. Indeed, it often comes as a surprise to recall that the original pressure for the containment of big business by antitrust laws came not from labor or from "the public," but from small businessmen who were being driven to the wall.

Here too is unmistakable evidence of a decline in the power of big business—not, as in the case with labor, because of a growth in the countervailing power of the other party, but through the operation of laws such as the Fair Trade acts and the repeated strengthening of antitrust legislation. In some areas the elimination of small business under the pressure of big business continues—as, for example, in the independent grocery field, or with independent filling stations or drug stores. But the elimination takes place under the aegis of impersonal market forces and rarely, if ever, through the deliberate maneuvering of the larger companies. Typically, when a merger takes place between a small firm and a large one these days, it is not because the small firm has been forced to sell out but because there are substantial tax advantages of which the small businessman is eager to take advantage.

Small business still continues to manifest a latent anti-big business sentiment that bubbles up from time to time—for instance, in the revolt of the General Motors dealers or in the recurrent discovery by the Small Business Committee of Congress that the large companies get the overwhelming bulk of defense contracts. But such sporadic and mild protests aside, it is surely fair to maintain that the fiery anti-big business feelings prevalent fifty years ago among the small business community have today largely been dissipated.

It is less easy to make an unambiguous finding with respect to the third traditional target of big business power in the marketplace—the consumer. Certainly the consumer is much more ardently wooed than in the public-be-damned days, when it was said that he was born to the profit of the Milk Trust and died to the profit of the Coffin Trust. The big corporation today falls all over itself in its efforts to depict itself as the servant of the public. It must be said, however, that this ardent wooing is sometimes accompanied by breach of promise. Cagily phrased advertisements, dubious testimonials, outright deception in television "demonstrations," glittering packaging and shoddy contents are all too familiar elements in consumer selling. From time to time these instances make the newspapers, as when the Federal Trade Commission found that General Foods was charging more, per unit of weight, for its "economy-sized" packages than for its regular packages. But leafing through the pages of *Consumer Reports* at any time hardly leaves one with a sense of overwhelming corporate solicitude for the consumer.

If it is uncertain that the big corporation really caters to the modern customer with all the zeal that it advertises, so it is also uncertain that the consumer is no longer plucked on the market as badly as ever in the old days. Long-term comparisons are difficult to make, since the higher bite of corporate tax laws has brought an increasing sophistication to corporate accounting, and many profits that were once proudly announced are now "charged off" in various ways. But certainly there is no evidence that corporate profit margins as a whole have declined over the past half century. Indeed, in certain lines of goods profit margins are higher than ever. General Motors, for example, makes almost as much profit per car as it pays out for wages on the car, and for every dollar of increased labor costs since 1947 it has raised automobile prices by about $3.75. Its profit "target" is 20 percent on capital *after* taxes—on the assumption that it will operate its plants only thirty-six weeks out of fifty-two. This goes a long way to explain its after-tax profits for 1965 of $2,125,606,440.

The only force that can be counted on to keep consumer prices down is competition. It is arguable that product competition has increased since the days of the breakup of the Trusts, but no one would contend that price competition has sharpened. Hence, while the power of the big company vis-à-vis the consumer may be more genteelly used, it has not noticeably diminished nor does it seem likely to do so.

Thus if we conclude that the exploitative capability of big business toward labor and small business has weakened, this cannot be echoed with respect to the consumer. But that does not yet fully satisfy our inquiry. For everyone knows that market exploitation, however bad, is not all of what we mean by the power of big business within society. In fact what the words usually bring to mind are not so much these instances of market abuse, but larger and subtler kinds of influence—for example, business's use of the national government to create new domains of private profits, as in the enormous landgrabs of the railroad era, or the insinuation of business ends into foreign policy, such as the banana republic diplomacy that once made the world safe for United Fruit, or the blind deference to business views characteristic of the 1920's when Calvin Coolidge could say in earnest that the business of America was business.

It is not easy to assay the trend of this varied and immensely important form of power. Certainly, when we are alerted to some new insinuation of business influence into the Pentagon, or when we remember the tidelands oil steal, or when we learn about the perversion of the income tax for the benefit of the very rich, we cannot airily dismiss the influence of big business on the nation's affairs as a thing of the past. Anyone who has read Robert Engler's *Politics of Oil,* or who has followed the course of efforts to write a stronger Pure Food and Drug Act, or to require admonitory labeling of cigarettes, or who has probed into the operations of the Federal Communications Commission or the Federal Power Commission, or who notes the parade of business chieftains into the White House, knows that big business continues to exercise a very important influence on the formulation and administration of the nation's policies, including not least those policies that are supposed to regulate business itself. Of all the interest groups in the nation, no other is so potent as business.

Nevertheless, I would hazard the opinion that the power of big business to shape legislation or to have its way in the determination of national policy is on the wane. What one needs here, above all, is a sense of historic perspective that will enable us to weigh the present degree of business penetration with that characteristic of the 1920's and the 1900's. One has to judge the ease of access to the President and Congress by business leaders, the weight accorded their opinions, the countervailance of nonbusiness institutions, and not least the ability of newspapers and broadcasting stations to influence electoral opinion today and in the days of T. R. Roosevelt, Taft, Harding, Coolidge, Hoover. Here precise judgments are largely impossible and subjective evaluations inescapable. I can only say that my own judgment leads me to believe that business has experienced a considerable diminution in its ability to influence the immediate course of events, comparing the pre-Depression era with our own.

I would rest this case not alone on a subjective estimate of the degree of business influence in general, but also on some observable aspects of American society. One of these we have noted already—the slowdown in the rate of expansion of big business within the economy and the change in the character of its leadership. Another perhaps even more important development, to which we must now pay heed, is the rise within our society of new elites, whose importance in and competence for the direction of national affairs is clearly on the increase, compared with that of the business elite.

One of these new groups is the military, whose emergence into national prominence during the Second World War has never been followed by a normal eclipse. The military forces of the nation not only constitute an enormous semi-independent bureaucracy aggregating half the employees in the federal government (which does not include the three million in the armed forces), but high-ranking military personnel have increasingly emerged as counselors of the over-all political, as well as military, strategy of the United States.

Ever since President Eisenhower's surprising reference to the "military-industrial" complex there has been considerable discussion as to the relationship of business to the military machine. There is little doubt that a military-industrial-political interpenetration of interests exists, to the benefit of all three. Yet in this alliance I have seen no suggestion that the industrial element is the dominant one. It is the military or the political branch that commands, and business that obeys; and although company officials have offered lavish entertainment, high post-retirement positions, and other inducements to the political and the military, the role of business in the entire defense effort is essentially one of jockeying for favor rather than initiating policy.

A second elite that has risen relatively to the business elite is the professional expert—the advisor from the academic world, and in particular from the areas of social and natural science. In part this is also a by-product of the enormous increase in military activity—between 1950 and 1965, research and development expenditures by the Department of Defense grew from $652 million to $7 billion, research in space exploration from $54 million to $5 billion; and in atomic energy from $221 million to $1.5 billion.

But the tremendous jump in the demand for scientists was not confined to military or quasi-military purposes alone. The National Science Foundation spent $1 million in 1952 and $204 million in 1965; health, education, and welfare research budgets grew from $40 million to $796 million in the same years. These figures reflect not only the explosive growth of technical expertise within the United States but its virtual pre-emption by nonbusiness sectors.

The direction of this vast flow of research effort is now a matter of the highest national priority—but it is a matter that is largely determined by the military, political, and scientific communties, rather than by the business community.

A third elite, also rising rapidly in national prominence and importance, is the government administrator. The moving force here, of course, is the increasing importance of the public sector in the operation of the over-all economy. Between 1950 and 1960, for example, private enterprise accounted for only one out of every ten new jobs that were created in the economy. All the rest were generated by the public or the private not-for-profit sectors (university, hospital, philanthropic, etc.). Today a third of the labor force works for some employer other than a private businessman, compared with only 15 percent in 1929. This very considerable displacement of the business world clearly points to a corresponding shift in the importance and influence of public officials in the determination of the course of national affairs.

Thus the years since the Great Depression have seen the rise of at least three new elites to challenge the previously uncontested dominance of the business elite—four, if we add the much larger role played by labor unions. The military, the professional advisor from the field of physics, medicine, economics, foreign affairs, the career administrator in the fields of agriculture, public health, transportation, housing, collective bargaining, and the labor union officialdom are among them responsible for the delineation and review of programs affecting the social, economic, and political life of the nation to an unrecognizably larger degree than before the Depression. What is more, I think we can expect their influence relative to that of business to increase still further.

The reason is not far to seek. If the nation at large were to draw up a list of those matters that appeared of the greatest urgency for the future, I suspect that on every list—including those of businessmen—we would find defense, economic stability and growth, foreign relations, poverty, civil rights, urban renewal, education, unemployment, mass transport, population control, and the like. The lists would undoubtedly have different priorities and each list might not include the items of every other, but there would be, I think, a wide consensus as to the most important challenges facing the nation in the future. There would also be a striking common denominator to the problems on the list. All of them are problems in which the initiatory impulse, the financial support, the essential policy determinations, and the day-to-day guidance of programs would have to come largely from nonbusiness elites. To put it differently, the thing at which businessmen are best —the production and sale of marketable goods and services —is no longer the thing that stands at the head of America's list of needs. No doubt for an effective discharge of our nonbusiness programs we depend on a vigorous productive foundation, but that requires not so much the indiscriminate encouragement of output as its redirection.

Thus it seems to me that the trends of the present, which are far from halted, portend a continuation of the general elevation of nonbusiness elites and a general compression of the influence of business leadership itself. To put my prognostication as concretely as possible, I expect to see fewer big businessmen in positions of power in Washington and more educators, career administrators, scientists, or soldiers; to see fewer big businessmen as trustees of universities or on the boards of the largest foundations, and more of the new men of influence there; to hear less about the sanctity of foreign investment and more about economic development; to find less attention paid to the rhetoric of laissez faire and more to that of Neo-Keynesianism and Input-Output Tables. In a word, I believe that the slowly fading presence of the big businessman as an originator of policy or as a counselor in the determination of foreign and domestic affairs will fade further, and that his place will be increasingly taken by new men, largely from nonbusiness backgrounds.

Always, in long-run historical comparisons of this sort one runs the risk of overstating the case. Hence let me repeat my earlier emphasis on the power that big business still commands. Of all the various centers of influence and direction within America, the business community is still unquestionably the single most important as regards the shaping of national policy. Nonetheless, I think it is an unavoidable conclusion, once one takes a line of sight into the past, that this power, however formidable, is markedly less than was the case in the not so very distant era prior to the Great Depression.

Do we conclude, then, that the limits of business power within American society are shrinking? If we ask the question in terms of the ability of the big corporation to exploit others on the marketplace, I think the answer is clearly Yes, its power has been substantially curtailed. If we ask in terms of the ability of big businessmen to work their will with the governing authorities or to turn national policy to pecuniary advantage, I would answer more carefully that, Yes, I think this power is now less than it was in the past and that the trend of things seems to portend a further constriction in business influence of this kind.

Yet, curiously, that does not quite exhaust the matter. For, while the specific powers of big business are being compressed, from another vantage point the position of business within society was never more solidly entrenched. By this I mean that its legitimacy is now virtually complete, its acceptance without exception. For perhaps the first time in American history there is no longer any substantial intellectual opposition to the system of business nor any serious questioning of its economic privileges and benefits. In the past a few small but articulate groups, mainly comprising intellectuals and fringes of the labor movement, have imagined a New Order that would sweep away the Old, and have often placed the business system on the defensive.

Today even these erstwhile dissenters have largely given up all thought of passage to a New Society, and exert their energies toward the improvement of things within the given economic structure. As a result, capitalism has become the virtually unchallenged order to which the ambitions of future American society must accommodate themselves.

It is true, of course, that business *feels* anything but unchallenged. The gradual constriction of its former untrammeled freedom, the frequent reminders that other elites are now its equal or even its superiors in the determination of national events, gives rise within the business world to a pervasive unease and to forebodings of unwelcome change, of "creeping socialism."

Yet from the position of one outside the business system, the encroachments on the prerogatives of business can be seen as anything but anticapitalist in their intent or effect. The measures that have been forced down the throats of business have been, without exception, measures designed to protect and preserve the main institutions of the business system from self-destruction. Certainly whatever sentiments that new elites may hold, they are not antibusiness. Neither the scientist, the military, the professional academician, nor the government official has any thoughts of nationalization, or of extensive decommercialization, or of far-reaching changes in the tax or inheritance laws. On the contrary, a general acquiesence of the business system, when it does not descend to outright sycophancy, describes the general attitude of the nonbusiness leaders. At most the ideas of the new elites imply a kind of managed capitalism in which the great corporations, maintained intact, would be coordinated within the national effort by some sort of "permissive planning." But it is in itself indicative of the general consensus that even the formulation of so mild a goal comes as something of a shock, and that most of the new elites would plead that they had no objective other than a day-to-day "pragmatic" approach to the nation's problems.

In our next essay we shall see that these elites may well someday develop an independent orientation, and formulate a program for American society that transcends the limits imposed by the present system. But at least within the time span of a generation or so, the development of such a trans-capitalist program is highly unlikely. We live in a civilization in which the limitations of a society built on the struggle to amass private wealth are never mentioned. In such a society centers of wealth, both personal and institutional, must perforce be great centers of influence. However much the new elites may crowd into positions of direct control, the traditional attraction of wealth, the admiration for the great corporation, and the deference to the successful businessman are likely to continue to dominate our social mores for a long while.

Then, too, in a business society the continuous entrance of business ideas into the general awareness constitutes an immense force for the preservation of the status quo. Partly by the appeal of direct "institutional" advertising (although this is no doubt the weakest of all methods), partly by the friendly image of business generally portrayed by the means of communication, but mostly by the never-ending exposure to the assumptions of business and the virtual absence of any serious questioning of its premises, it becomes almost impossible not to think in terms compatible with the business system. The military man as well as the scientist, the public administrator as well as the labor leader, grow up in a world that basks in the business sun, that is raised and nurtured by the hand of business, that turns to business for its daily wherewithal, that engages in business for its advancement, and that looks to business for its central form of organization; and it is little wonder that to disbelieve in the fundamental arrangements of the system, or to advocate radical curtailments of its privileges, or to espouse alternative means of arranging for production and distribution, employment and remuneration, advancement and retirement, far, far exceeds the reach of mind of all but a very few.

If this prognostication is true, what does it portend for the future? Within the next generation or so, the answer would seem to depend on two factors. One of these is the ideology that will come to represent the "central" business position, and thereby also serve to delineate the boundaries of what is thinkable and doable by nonbusiness groups in society. We have already seen that the ideology of the big business center has moved appreciably from its position in the past, and there is the chance—and I think a good chance—that it will continue to move further. The pressures for "pragmatic" changes, the continuous series of problems raised by a new technology and by an ever more crowded urban milieu, the hostile world environment, and not least the process of rationalization and intellectualization to which both Max Weber and Joseph Schumpeter referred as the great solvents of the spirit of our age, are all at work silently and ubiquitously, and can be expected to exert their corrosive effects within the business world as they will on the world at large.

Thus there would seem to be reason to hope that a more liberal business ideology, accepting rather than attempting to thwart the general currents of change of our time, will gradually replace the older ideology. This prospect—which, it must be emphasized, can be no more than conjectural—has very important implications. It is difficult to hold a sanguine view of the adaptive capabilities of the business system if its ruling ideas of society continue to be as parochial, uninformed, and inflexible as has been the case in the past, or indeed, as is still the case with a substantial portion of the business community today. Despite the shift in the central viewpoint of big business, the social and economic changes acceptable to it today are not yet such as to inspire much confidence for the future. Under the limits imposed by the present reach of business thought, the prospect is still for a society of narrow ambitions and small achievements, a society in which we belatedly repair old social ills and ungenerously attend to new ones.

Such need not be the case, however, under the more liberal wing of business opinion—for example, that expressed by Thomas Watson in his McKinsey lectures. A reasonably free use of government's economic powers to promote growth and stability, a substantial widening of the welfare structure, a generally open attitude toward social problems at home and political problems abroad, distinguishes this view and makes it possible to hope for a range of thought and action that far exceeds that of the older school. Thus the gradual accession of the liberal philosophy of business could exert a marked effect on the vitality and creativity of the business system itself, with long-run consequences that could be very great indeed.

Yet that is not quite the whole of the matter. The business ideology, important determinant of the near-term future that it is, is still not the sole arbiter of that future. There remains a second determinant in the structure and characteristics of the business system itself, a determinant stemming from the limitations that the institutions and privileges of capitalism impose on ideology. Adaptive change may be held short of these limits by a recalcitrant business community, but it is not likely to exceed them even under the most permissive business outlook.

Thus, within the timespan of our lives and perhaps of those of our children, the potential evolution of capitalism must be seen as a limited one, a journey within boundaries that, like those of a great desert, can neither be precisely drawn nor easily crossed. Hence the question to which we must now turn is an investigation of what those indeterminate but formidable boundaries are, and of what possibilities are open and denied to American capitalism within the general limits we can ascribe to it.

☆

PART II
THE LIMITS
OF AMERICAN
CAPITALISM

☆

☆ 1 ☆

Our first essay was concerned with the business system as it exists in the present; our second will be concerned with capitalism as it may exist in the future. The change in our direction of inquiry necessarily involves us in a shift of emphasis from description to speculation, but the shift does not represent a leap from hard fact to sheer fancy. As the reader has already learned, there is a substantial and inextricable element of speculation in the effort to sort out the "facts" of the empirical present; in like fashion, if the act of prognostication is to carry any plausibility at all, it must

65

rest on premises that are clearly visible as current realities. But what does it mean to try to establish the "limits" for capitalism in the future? Perhaps we can shed an initial light on the question if we imagine asking some perceptive observer in, say, thirteenth-century France, what were the limits of feudalism? Our observer might be hard put to find an answer, particularly if he looked about him at the striking variety of forms that feudalism assumed in the various domains of Europe. Yet undoubtedly we could have suggested an answer to him that would have sounded reasonable. It is that certain kinds of economic and social change were unimaginable—indeed impossible—in thirteenth-century France because they would have implied the establishment of some totally different form of social organization. To take one central instance, it would have been impossible to have replaced the traditional ties, established customs, and fixed obligations by which the manorial economy hung together with some radically different system, such as the cash markets that were already disrupting the settled tenor of feudal economic life, because a change of this dimension would have critically undermined the power of the lord and elevated out of all proportion that of the parvenu class of merchants.

Thus one meaning we can give to the idea of "limits" is very simple: It is those boundaries of change that would so alter the functional base of a society, or the structure of privilege built on that base, as to displace a given social order by a new one. To be sure, the exact line as to what constitutes a vital infringement on the body of a society is by no means easy to draw, and it is precisely here, at the margin of change, that ideology plays its decisive role in admitting or excluding particular alterations in a social structure. Nonetheless, if we look beyond this uncertain border, it is usually not too difficult to describe those changes that would, as of any moment, constitute an assault on the core structures of function and privilege, and which are, for that reason, impossible for a society to make.

In terms of the immediate subject of our essay, this draws the broad limits of American capitalism in the last third of the twentieth century with reasonable fixity. To take a few examples: It is certainly beyond the present limits of capitalism to replace the guiding principle of production for profit by that of production for use—which is to say, it is impossible to redirect the main flow of economic effort away from the pull of market considerations to areas established by public policy decisions. It is impossible to nationalize the great corporations or the private ownership of the means of mass communication, with the result that corporate power will continue to exert its massive conservative influence and the channels of mass communication will continue to be used mainly as sales and propaganda instruments for the business interest rather than as agencies for public enlightenment. Again, it is impossible to end the concentration of private wealth, so that the existing influence of huge family fortunes such as the Rockefellers or the Texas oil estates can be expected to continue. One can debate whether all or any of these or similar changes are desirable, but there is little point in debating whether they are realizable. Barring only some disaster that would throw open the gates to a radical reconstruction of society, they are not.

What we have established thus far, however, is only the first and most obvious answer to the question of what we mean by the "limits" of social change. For if we now return to the thirteenth century we could imagine suggesting to our medieval observer another approach to the idea of feudal limits. Rather than pointing out to him the contemporary incompatibility of the market system with thirteenth-century practices and notions, we might be able to show him the immense long-term historical momentum of the emergent forces of the monetized economy. Indeed, we might even be able to bring him to see that by the end of another four or five centuries feudalism would have virtually disappeared, and that an economic organization of society once incompatible with feudalism would have triumphed over it.

From such a perspective, the task of delineating the limits of feudalism becomes a different one. It is no longer to declare what is impossible, but rather to ascertain what is, after all, possible—no longer to discover what cannot be done in the short run, but to explore what *can* be done, and how, in doing it, the social structure may slowly and subtly alter, making possible still further change in the future.

It need hardly be said that one cannot project such a long evolutionary—or possibly revolutionary—view in close detail. Just as the restrictive limits of change must leave room for an uncertain margin, so the extensive limits of change can indicate little more than the general direction and the approximate final destination of social advance. The precise route to be taken, the pace of progress, the roadblocks where the invading forces of a new society may be temporarily halted or even thrown back—all this surpasses any power of analysis we now have.

But the grand line of march is not beyond our ability to foresee. Looking back at thirteenth-century France, we can see how defenseless were its castle walls against the insinuating influence of the market system; and in our own time, looking to the future, it is not impossible to identify powerful forces making for slow but equally penetrative changes in the midst of American capitalism. Thus it should be feasible to explore the limits of capitalism in America, not alone in terms of those changes that cannot now be accommodated by the business system but also in terms of those forces that are carrying capitalism, like feudalism in an earlier day, in directions that will eventually alter its social and economic structure beyond anything that would today be possible to achieve.

☆ 2 ☆

We shall be speaking at length of the limits of the business system and of the forces pressing against it. But before
we proceed to this central theme, there is an aspect of the
process to which we must direct our attention. This is the
nature of the resistance to social change offered by societies in general, and in particular that offered by a capitalist
society.

Why do societies resist change? A full explanation of
social inertia must reach deep into the psychological and
technical underpinnings of the human community. But in
the context of our present concern we need not delve to
such depths. For in the process of gradual social adjustment
it is clear enough where to look for the main sources of the
resistance to change. They are to be found in the structure
of privilege inherent in all societies, against which the pressures of change pose their threats.

Privilege is not an attribute we are accustomed to stress
when we consider the construction of a social order, in
particular our own. Yet it is obvious enough that not only
our society but all societies award to certain groups or
classes disproportionate shares of wealth, power, and prestige. There is little difficulty in seeing the nature of the
privileges incorporated in the structure of feudalism, or in

the kingdoms of antiquity, with their castes, slaves, and priestly or noble upper strata. The difficulty only arises when we are asked to consider the nature of privilege in our own social system.

When pressed, we are, of course, aware of the core institutions of privilege in capitalism—the right to reap private benefit from the use of the means of production and the right to utilize the dynamic forces of the marketplace for private enrichment. The element of privilege in these institutions and working arrangements, however—that is, their operative result in favoring certain individuals and groups —is usually passed over in silence in favor of their purely functional aspects. Thus the institution of private property is ordinarily explained as being no more than a convenient instrumentality for the efficient operation of an economic system, or the market elements of Land, Labor, and Capital as purely neutral "factors of production" whose technically efficient cooperation is achieved under the governance of impersonal forces.

Now these institutions and relationships do indeed fulfill the purposes for which they are advertised. But this is not the only use they have. Land, Labor, and Capital are not just functional parts of a mechanism that can be assembled or disassembled, improved or altered at will, but are categories of social existence that bring vast differences in life chances with them. It is not just Labor on the one hand and Land or Capital on the other; it is the Bronx on the one hand and Park Avenue on the other. Similarly, private property is not merely a pragmatic arrangement devised for the facilitation of production, but a social institution whose existence and function bring to some members of the community a style of life qualitatively different from that afforded to the community in general. In a word, the operation of capitalism as *functional* system results in a structure of wealth and income characteristic of capitalism as a *system of privilege*—a structure in which the top 2 percent of all American families own between two-thirds and three-quarters of all corporate stock, and where the top 2 percent of all income receivers enjoy incomes roughly ten times larger than the average received within the nation as a whole.

The mere presence of these concentrations of wealth or large disparities of income does not in itself differentiate the system of privilege under capitalism from those of most other societies in history. Rather, what marks off our system is that wealth and income within capitalism are not mainly derived from noneconomic activity, such as war, plunder, and extortionate taxation, but arise from the activity of marketers or the use of property by its owners.

This mixture of the functional and the privileged aspects of capitalism has a curious but important political consequence. It is that privilege under capitalism is much less "visible," especially to the favored groups, than privilege under other systems. The upper classes in feudalism or in the states of antiquity, for example, were keenly alive to the gulf that separated them from the lower classes, and perfectly open about the need for preserving the distance and differences between the classes. The upper groups under capitalism, on the other hand, are typically unaware that the advantages accruing to them from following the paths of the market economy constitute in any fashion a "privileged" course of action. Nothing more astonishes or perplexes a businessman than to be asked to consider the famous quotation of John Stuart Mill that bears repetition here:

> *Even what a person has produced by his individual toil, unaided by anyone, he cannot keep, unless by permission of society. Not only can society take it from him, but individuals could and would take it from him, if society only remained passive; if it didn't interfere* en masse, *or employ and pay people for the purpose of preventing him from being disturbed in the possession.*

This lack of self-awareness is rendered even more acute by virtue of another differentiating characteristic of privilege under capitalism. It is that privilege is limited to the advantages inherent in the economic structure of society. That is, the same civil and criminal law, the same duties in war and peace, apply to both economically privileged and unprivileged—although it hardly need be said that a considerable gulf separates the application of the "identical" laws and duties as between the rich and the poor. But it would be a mistake to concentrate on this differential application of the law as being of the essence. Rather, one must contrast the single system of law and obligation under capitalism—however one-sidedly administered—with the *differing* systems that apply to privileged and unprivileged in other societies. Indeed, it is worth recalling that the very word for privilege stems from *privata lex*, or the private law that protected the favored classes of earlier societies.

The divorce of economic from political or social privilege brings up the obvious fact that at least in democratic societies like America the privileged distribution of economic rewards is exposed to the corrective efforts of the democratic electorate.

There is indeed such an opposition of interests, and we can trace numerous curtailments in economic privilege to the triumphs of a political egalitarianism over the claims of economic preferment. The question is, however, why the structure of privilege has remained so relatively intact, despite its long exposure to the potentially leveling influences of the majority.

In part we can trace the answer to the very "invisibility" of privilege we have just described—a fact that makes the identification of privilege unusually difficult. Then there is the further consideration that, as in all stable societies, the structure of privilege appears to the general public not as a special dispensation but as the natural order of things, with which their own interests and sentiments are identified. This is especially true under capitalism, where the privileges of wealth are open, at least in theory, and to some extent in practice, to all comers. Not least, of course, the over-all results of capitalism, particularly in America during the entire twentieth century and recently in Europe as well, have been sufficiently rewarding to hold anticapitalist sentiment to a relatively small segment of the population.

To emphasize the defense of privilege as the active source of resistance to social and economic change may appear so obvious as scarcely to be worth saying. Obvious or not, it is too often passed over in silence. It seems to me impossible to analyze the nature of the opposition to change without stressing the vulgar but central fact that every person who is rich under capitalism is a beneficiary of its inherent privileges, and that the defense of wealth constitutes an enormously powerful motivation for most men.

To be sure, there are other motives that impel various groups within capitalism, including capitalists, and there are as well slow changes in the substratum of motivations, comparable to those that have already produced the corporate manager in place of the tycoon. Yet, taking the American system as it now exists, it seems fair to assert that the chance to own and acquire wealth constitutes a primary —perhaps even a dominating—social motivation for most men, including the new elites; and that those who enjoy or aspire to these privileges will not readily acquiesce to changes that will substantially lessen their chances of gaining them.

☆ 3 ☆

The touchstone of privilege provides an indispensable key when we now return to the main theme of our inquiry. If it does not give us an exact calculus by which to compute what changes will and will not be acceptable, it does give us an angle of entry, a point of view, without which attempts to cope with the problem of social change are apt to have no relevance at all.

Take, for example, the problem of the poverty that now afflicts some 30 to 40 million Americans. It is plain enough that the coexistence of poverty with the general affluence of the American upper classes brings the critical element of privilege directly to the fore. Yet the precise way in which the defense of privilege bears on the fact of poverty needs more than cursory examination.

One alleged cause of poverty has always been wage exploitation—that is, the systematic diversion to property owners of workers' income. There is clearly an element of truth in part of this contention, in that the income of the favored groups in capitalism does indeed stem from institutions that divert income from the community at large into the channels of dividends, interest, rent, monopoly returns, etc. What is by no means clear, however, is that the amount of this diversion, if redistributed among the masses, would spell the difference between their poverty and their well-being. On the contrary, it is now generally acknowledged, including by most Marxists, that the level of wages reflects workers' productivity more than any other single factor, and that this productivity in turn is primarily determined by the quantity and the quality of the capital equipment of the economic system.

Certainly the productivity of the great mass of workers under capitalism has steadily increased, and so have their real wages. Today, for example, industrial workers in America cannot be classified as "poor" by prevailing absolute standards, if we take $4,000 a year as designating a level of minimum adequacy for a small family (some studies of poverty set this level at only $3,000). For 1959, the last year for which figures exist, the median yearly incomes of broad categories of workers was as follows:

MEDIAN ANNUAL EARNINGS OF EXPERIENCED MALE WORKERS,
UNITED STATES, 1959

	All ages, white and nonwhite	Ages 35 to 44 white	nonwhite
Craftsmen and foremen	$5240	$5795	$3885
Sales workers	4987	6325	4010
Clerical workers	4785	5505	4630
Operatives	4299	5075	3495
Service workers	3310	4610	2970
Farmers and farm managers	2169	2945	945
Farm laborers	1066	2020	975

The figures tell a clear enough story. Wage poverty is clearly present in capitalism, but it is primarily restricted to the agricultural areas and to the lowest categories of skills in the service trades. No small part of it is accounted for by discrimination against Negros, and by the really shocking levels of income of Negro farm and service labor. On the other hand, the proportion of the labor force that is afflicted with this poverty is steadily diminishing. Farmers, farm managers, and farm laborers together accounted for only 8 percent of the labor force in 1959, and will probably constitute only 5 percent within a decade. The nonfarm common laborer, who constituted over 12 percent of the working force in 1900, makes up only 5 percent of it today and will be a still smaller percentage tomorrow.

There remains, nevertheless, the question of how much the existing level of wages could be increased if the categories of capitalist privilege did not exist. Since it is difficult to estimate accurately the total amount of "privileged" income under capitalism (unless we contrast the existing distribution of income with an absolutely flat equality), let us take as its convenient representation the sum total of all corporate profits before tax. In the mid 1960's, these profits exceeded $70 billion a year. If this sum were distributed equally among the 70 million members of the work force, the average share would be $1,000. For the lowest paid workers, such as migrant farm laborers, this would represent an increase in annual incomes of 100 percent or more—an immense gain. For the average industrial worker, however, the gain would be in the neighborhood of 20 to 25 percent, certainly a large increase but not one that would fundamentally alter his living standards. More realistically, if the redirection of privileged income were confined to dividends (rather than all profits), the average distribution as of the mid 1960's would be of the order of $250—an increase in income for the poorest workers of some 20 to 30 percent, and for the industrial worker of only about 5 to 6 percent.

Thus, in so far as the institutions of capitalism constitute a drain upon nonprivileged groups, it can be fairly said that, however great the benefits of these institutions to those who gain from them, they are only marginally responsible for any inadequacy in the prevailing general level of income. Individual companies may indeed be capable of vastly improving the lot of their workers—General Motors, to repeat a figure from the previous essay, makes nearly as much gross profit on a car as it pays out in wages, and "could" therefore virtually double its wages. But for the economy as a whole no such large margin of redistribution is possible. The privileges received under the system do not substantially depress the level of average income, nor would their removal permit them to be substantially increased. Thus, so long as the defense of these privileges does not result in substantially *increasing* the share of national income accruing to the privileged elements of the nation, it seems fair to conclude that the level of material well-being under capitalism is limited mainly by the levels of productivity it can reach. If the trend of growth of the past century is continued—and there is no reason to believe this impossible—the average level of real wages for industrial labor should double in another two to three decades. This would bring average earnings to a level of about $10,-000 and would effectively spell the abolition of wage poverty, under any definition.

Thus the institutions of privilege can be seen to play only a minor role in depressing the level of wages. But this conclusion does not close our investigation into the relationship between poverty and privilege, but rather directs it toward what is now revealed as the principal cause of poverty. This is the fact that large groups within the population—the aged, the handicapped, the sick, the unemployed, the castaways in rural backwaters—have no active tie into the market economy and must therefore subsist at the very meager levels to which nonparticipants in the work process are consigned.

So far as the great majority of these poor are concerned, there is only one way that their condition can be quickly alleviated, but that one way would be very effective indeed. This is to redistribute to them income earned or received by more favored members of the community. To some extent this is already done. In 1963, 7.5 million individuals (about one-fifth of the poor) received federal, state, or local benefits totaling $4.7 billion, or a little over $600 each. In addition, an unknown number received some degree of help from private charity, amounting in all to less than $1.5 billion.

This sum must be compared with the amount needed to

raise the 35 million individuals whose incomes fall below levels of decency to an average of some $3,000 per family or $1,500 per individual. A program with this modest objective would require an additional $11.5 billion above the public assistance that is now received. Such a sum would amount to roughly a seventh of corporate profits before tax. Alternatively, shared among the 11 or 12 million families who constitute the top 20 percent of the nation's income receivers, it would require an additional tax of roughly $1,000 on incomes that average $16,000, thereby raising the average tax liabilities of families in this bracket from $2,300 to $3,300.

It need hardly be said that "curing poverty" involves a good deal more than the transfer of a subsistence income from the rich to the poor. Elaborate rebuilding of slum areas, extensive training, special education, and intensive medical care will all be needed before the culture of poverty melts away; and these supplemental programs will be much more expensive than the minimum program of a dole. The fact remains, however, that the dole itself *would* effectively eliminate the immediate need that affronts anyone with eyes to see and the strength of will to investigate the ruined areas of the cities, and that the failure to institute such a program cannot be laid to any factor other than the general unwillingness of those who enjoy higher incomes to share their good fortune with those who do not. As Adam Walinsky has very aptly put it: "The middle class knows that the economists are right when they say that poverty could be eliminated if we only will it; they simply do not will it."

Thus the defense of the existing structure of privilege must bear its full blame for the failure to eradicate poverty in America today. To what prospect does that conclusion then lead when we inquire into the possibility of eliminating poverty within the next generation or so?

In the short run the outlook is not very hopeful. Given the prevailing conservative temper of the business community, the temptations of luxury consumption, and the general lack of concern in a nation lulled by middle-class images of itself, it is doubtful that bold or far-reaching programs of social rescue will be launched within the next decade or two. Looking at the present extent of the problem—at the numbers of people who need to have their life circumstances radically altered and at the acres of real estate that must be remodeled from the ground up—it seems unlikely that very great changes will be made within ten or twenty years, even at double or treble the present rate of expenditure. During the next generation, at least, the slums will still be with us, the Negroes will continue to constitute a depressed class, the old will continue to eke out a thin living.

Yet, of all the problems confronting capitalism, poverty seems the least likely to be permanently blocked by the resistance of privilege. Here, two elements combine to offer a chance for a long-run fundamental improvement in the lot of the poor. One of these is the availability of a relatively painless source of finance for a massive social program in the steadily rising revenues of the federal government. Tax receipts are now growing at the rate of some $6 billion a year as a consequence of the growth of national output, and this flow of funds to the government will increase over the future. For some years these receipts may be absorbed by higher arms expenditures, but assuming that full-scale war is averted, sooner or later the arms budget must level off. Thereafter the funds will become available for use either in the form of tax reductions—an operation which normally favors the well-to-do—or as the wherewithal for a major assault on the slums, etc. In this choice between the claims of privilege and those of social reform, the critical push may well come from the new elites rising within capitalism, especially those from government and academic backgrounds. Secondly, the gradual liberalization of the business ideology, to which we are hopefully looking forward, should also ease opposition to measures such as these that patently improve the quality of society without substantially affecting its basic institutions of privilege.

It is idle to predict when Harlem will be reconstructed and Appalachia reborn, since so much depends on the turn of events in the international arena. Yet it seems to me that the general dimensions of the problem make it possible to envisage the substantial alleviation—perhaps even the virtual elimination—of poverty, partly through income transfers and partly through the creation of a more benign environment, within the limits of capitalism three or four decades hence, or possibly even sooner.

The elimination of poverty is, however, only part of a larger problem within capitalism—the problem of income distribution. Hence, we must now look to the other end of the income scale, and ask what are the chances that capitalism will alter the moral anomalies of wealth as well as those of poverty.

Here it is not so easy to foresee a change in the operational results of the system of privilege. Since the 1930's the political intent of the public has clearly been to bring about some lessening of the concentration of income that goes to the very rich and some diminution of the enclaves of family wealth that have passed intact from one generation to the next. Thus we have seen the introduction of estate taxes that levy imposts of about one-third on net estates of only $1 million, and of fully half on net estates of $5 million; and these rates have been supplemented by measures to prevent the tax-free passage of wealth before death by gift.

Since the enactment of these taxes in the mid-1930's a full generation has passed, and we would therefore expect to see some impact of the legislation in a significant lowering of the concentration of wealth among the top families. Instead we find that the share held by the top families has decreased only slightly—from 33 percent of all personal wealth in 1922 to 29 percent in 1953 (the last year for which such calculations exist). Moreover, most of whatever dilution these figures indicate has been due to a widening base of small holdings of government bonds, savings accounts, and the like. The concentration of stock—the single most important medium for the investment of large wealth—has shown no tendency to decline since 1922 (despite the great increase in small stockholders), and seems in fact to have increased: the top 2 percent of families, who held just under two-thirds of all corporate stock in the 1920's, actually held more than three-quarters of all stock in 1953. Since these figures change somewhat erratically from year to year, however, it would be rash to interpret this as a "trend."

Equally recalcitrant before the egalitarian purposes of legislation is the flow of income to topmost groups. Legal tax rates on top incomes have risen from 54 percent under President Hoover to over 90 percent in the 1940's and early 1950's, and to 72 percent in the mid-1960's. The presumed higher incidence of taxes at the peak of the income pyramid has, however, been subverted by innumerable stratagems of trust, family sharing of income, capital gains, deferred compensation, or other means of tax avoidance or outright tax evasion. At its worst this has led to grotesque results. In 1959, nineteen Americans had incomes over $5 million, but five paid no income tax whatsoever and not one of the rest paid in the top brackets to which their income presumably relegated them; while more recently one American received an income of $20 million and paid no tax on it at all.

That these are not merely individual instances is evidenced by a study of the Treasury income tax statistics. In 1960 the Chase Manhattan Bank advised the readers of its bimonthly newsletter that the differences between the legal and the effective rates of taxation, as revealed by these statistics, were as follows:

ADJUSTED GROSS INCOME	SCHEDULED RATES	ACTUAL RATES
Under $3,000	20%	19%
$10,000 to $14,999	25	20
$20,000 to $24,999	36	23
$50,000 to $99,999	55	38
$200,000 to $499,999	80	42
$1,000,000 and over	87	38

In other words, the actual percentage of income paid as tax by the average income receiver in the million-dollar bracket was *less* than that paid by a receiver in the $200,-000-to-$500,000 bracket, and for all intents and purposes no more than that paid by a recipient of an income one-twentieth that size.

There is no indication that this resistive capacity of the system of privilege is likely to weaken, at least not within the time span of a generation. Nor is there any sign that the "natural workings" of the system will lessen the flow of income to the top. The share of business profits in the gross national product has shown no tendency to decline over the past fifty years and may possibly have risen slightly, while dividend payments out of corporate earnings have also shown a rising tendency in recent years. The statistics of income distribution clearly show a regular drift of income *toward* the upper end of the income spectrum. Three percent of all income was received by income receivers in the $15,000-and-up brackets in 1947; in 1963, in terms of constant dollars, this percentage had grown to 8. If we take a still higher income bracket, we find that 2.4 percent of all income went to receivers in the $50,000-and-up bracket in 1947, and 4.0 percent in 1963—although in this case the figures must be adjusted for a fall in the purchasing power of money of slightly over a third between the two periods. Or, going higher still, we find the number of tax returns reporting an income of over $500,000 risen from 694 in 1951 to 1,041 in 1960 (the last year for which statistics are yet available).

Only very long-range alterations in the economic structure or in the prevailing ideology should be expected to work a fundamental transformation in this deep-seated attribute of capitalism. The determined perpetuation of large concentrations of private wealth is likely to continue—afflicting the social order with that peculiar irresponsibility that is the unhappy hallmark of the system. The power of wealth, as our essays have emphasized, is by no means the only source of power in America and may, in fact, be expected to decline. But the voice of money still speaks very loudly and the capacity of wealth to surmount the half-acquiescent opposition of a democratic political system promises that it will continue to resound in America for a long while to come. The deformations imposed on capitalism by poverty may very well be largely overcome within a generation or two; those imposed by wealth are much more liable to be with it still.

☆ 4 ☆

The maldistribution of income and the social problems that spring from it can no longer be said to constitute an issue that threatens the viability—although it may seriously jeopardize the social peace—of capitalism. This cannot be said, however, for a second problem that goes to the very heart of the ability of capitalism to continue as a social organization in good working order. This is the problem of the economic malfunction that has periodically racked capitalism over the last hundred years and that nearly caused its demise in the 1930's.

The persistent breakdowns of the capitalist economy, whatever their immediate precipitating factors, can all be traced to a single underlying cause. This is the anarchic or planless character of capitalist production. Essentially, capitalism malfunctions because the output of its individual firms is guided solely by the profitable opportunities open to each, without regard to the state of the market as a whole. As a result an economic short circuit results when-ever, for any number of possible reasons, the output of all firms fails to dovetail with the structure of demand, or when the production plans of the business community as a whole are not adequate to cope with the independently formulated savings plans of the community at large. These discrepancies between production and demand, or between saving and investment, can be more or less readily absorbed in an economy of small, flexible firms and readily liquidated capital assets. But in a milieu of huge enterprises and enormous fixed investments, miscalculations or imbalances carry the potential of a major disruptive impact.

Hence it is not surprising that reformers have long advo-cated planning as the remedy for capitalist depressions or stagnation. Indeed the idea of introducing conscious public control in place of the mindless private drives of the market has been a countertheme to capitalism of steadily mounting insistence—not alone from those who sought to replace capitalism by socialism but by those who wanted to pre-serve the main structure, while protecting it from its own destructive tendencies.

The trouble has been, however, that much of the plan-ning which its partisans have urged upon it has been in-compatible with the privileges of capitalism. Proposals to nationalize the core of heavy industry leaving the rest of the economy free, or to convert the biggest corporations into quasi-public utilities may have much to recommend them along strictly economic lines, but they all infringe the preserves of private property or of the market to a degree intolerable to the American business community. An economic transformation of capitalism of such magnitude that its big businesses become, in effect, public agencies is not a serious possibility for the foreseeable American future, barring a military or other calamity that would wreck the existing order.

This does not mean that planning is therefore ruled out and that capitalism is inherently doomed to suffer the instability characteristic of its past. On the contrary, a great deal of planning is virtually inevitable over the coming decades. The difference is that this planning is likely to be used in support of the main institutions of capitalism rather than as a means of transcending them.

What sort of planning is this like likely to be?

One main instrument is certain to be the use of the government's fiscal powers to maintain aggregate demand. Although we are still only in the early stages of experience with public demand-creation (through such devices as tax cuts or deliberately planned deficits), there is little doubt that a bold use of these mechanisms can remedy almost any likely shortfall of private demand, and can virtually guarantee a steady or rising level of total expenditure. Moreover, since demand-creation involves little or no interference with individual markets or business, it impinges little if at all on the preserves of privilege. Tax cuts, for example, are certain to be endorsed by the business and upper-income groups. Even additional spending, so long as it is within the established areas of public concern—arms, roads, schools, rivers and harbors, conservation, and perhaps social welfare—is apt to be welcome as a source of new business.

There remains, to be sure, a body of conservative resistance to the use of fiscal measures of a compensatory sort. The chairman of the Finance Committee of the United States Steel Company has used his company's annual report to inveigh against the dangers of deficit spending; and it is probable that his fears—compounded of an ignorance of public finance and a shrewd foreboding that the assumption of public economic responsibility, no matter how useful at the moment, is freighted with serious long-term implications—are shared by numerous others.

Yet it seems likely that this is a view of dwindling importance. A very considerable segment of business backed the controversial Kennedy tax cut, and the success of that policy should pave the way for further measures of the same kind. In addition, the nonbusiness elites, especially from the academic and government establishments, are strongly in favor of fiscal controls to buoy up the system, and their influence in securing the bold use of these measures may be very important or even decisive. Although there remain difficult problems in regard to demand-creation—on the one hand, of public education and, on the other, of learning to use the tools of fiscal policy skillfully—there seems a reasonable expectation that measures to safeguard the economy against the collapse of effective demand lie well within the ambit of capitalism today.

What is more difficult to judge is the extent to which capitalism will be able to go beyond the use of general fiscal planning into planning on a more detailed basis for the achievement of broad welfare objectives. Here the experience of Europe since the war is relevant. In nearly every nation of Europe we have seen the formulation of planning techniques that go considerably beyond the mere application of fiscal leverage, to the conscious "design" of the economic future. Yet these techniques with few exceptions do not directly abridge the prerogatives of the market or interfere with the capture of profits. Although the manner of planning varies from country to country, generally it consists in the development of cooperatively formulated national economic targets to which individual business firms voluntarily align their sights and to whose realization the government bends its over-all fiscal and monetary influence.

The very fact that European capitalism has taken this turn puts it beyond argument that a considerable amount of indirect planning is compatible with the privileges of capitalism. On the other hand the growth of European planning owes much to the particular traditions of European capitalism, including the more or less formalized structures of employers' federations and the pronounced "étatist" tradition in many states. The absence of comparable institutions and history makes doubtful the possibility of a wholesale transplantation of European forms of planning to America. Furthermore, unlike its sister capitalisms across the Atlantic, the United States has not become accustomed to the public ownership of transportation or utilities, or to a large public housing sector, or to the development of a strong system of public welfare. The non-defense public sector in America places a much smaller proportion of resources in public hands than in any nation of the European Community.

As a result of this lack of an étatist tradition the United States is severely handicapped in its attempts to introduce planning into the private terrain. For instance, in his study *Modern Capitalism* Andrew Schonfield tells how an attempt by the Council of Economic Advisors under President Kennedy merely to inquire into business investment intentions in a "Full Employment Perspective" evoked a storm of opposition from businessmen who felt that the exercise verged on becoming a serious foray into "planning." It was accordingly shelved but, as Schonfield acutely observes, the movement toward planning has nonetheless slowly proceeded, although under the generally approved title of "manpower planning" rather than the forbidden title of "economic planning."

The extent and speed with which American capitalism may move in the direction of detailed economic planning would thus seem to depend on two factors. One of them is, once again, the degree of liberalization of the business ideology. The other, perhaps of greater importance, is the urgency of the economic problems the future may bring. If, for example, the continued incursion of technology, coupled with a very large inflow of young people into the labor market, creates an employment crisis during the next decade—which is not unlikely, should the international scene quiet down—some form of industrial planning may emerge as a necessary instrument of social policy. In that case, policies designed to create employment through a substantial enlargement of public activities at state and local as well as federal levels or—looking further ahead—the designation of a civil sector, such as the rebuilding of the cities, as the peacetime equivalent of the military sector, might well show up as part of the practicable agenda.

It is not within our capacity to predict what combination of problems and ideas might bring about this closer engagement with planning. It is enough to conclude that a very considerable degree of planning *could* be integrated into capitalism without seriously infringing on the prerogatives of the great corporations or disturbing the rewards of the more favored groups in the economy. Certainly it does not seem unreasonable to suppose that at the end of another twenty years capitalism will have learned to live with a much more elaborate system of controls over the level of its total output and its grand division among various social purposes than exists at present.

As we have been at some pains to point out, capitalism can achieve considerable change within the boundaries imposed by its privileges. But it is important to recognize as well that there are also important limits beyond which it cannot go—at least within the foreseeable future. In a society that has no ideology other than that of the business system, planning cannot invade the domain of the market as the central organizing agency of society, or vitiate the rights of property as a claimant to income. These restrictions do not prevent considerable changes from being made in the external operating characteristics of the system, but they do enjoin certain other changes from being made in some of its internal attributes.

Primary among these is the continuing requirement that the economic participants in a capitalist world—even in a planned capitalist world—behave in the manner that is required of them if the market mechanism is to work. Briefly, they must act as "economic men," buying cheap and selling dear, allowing relative remunerations to weigh heavily on their choices of occupations or employments, setting acquisitive aims high in the hierarchy of life goals. These marketing traits are not merely pervasive private idiosyncrasies that can be dispensed with if they are no longer esteemed. They are integral to and necessary for the successful operation of the market system on which the privileges of capitalism ultimately rest.

In a setting of bare subsistence and newly risen entrepreneurs there is little difficulty in adducing the acquisitive behavior required to run a capitalist economy. But in a more advanced and affluent society where the primary drives of self-preservation begin to fail, the necessary marketing behavior must be sustained by supplementary motives of emulation and competitive striving. Thus the endless and relentless exacerbation of economic appetites in advanced capitalism—an exacerbation that does not draw the line at subjecting children to commercial propaganda or at interrupting its most serious presentations "to bring you this important message from our sponsor"—is not merely a surface aberration but a deeply rooted functional necessity to provide the motivations on which the market system depends.

Whether or not the more grotesque forms of commercialism can be subdued, this thralldom to an overwhelming economic imperative of sales and profits and this worship of a calculus of income are features of capitalism that cannot be eliminated by planning—at least not so long as the central institutions of the market system are allowed to remain. A planned capitalism of the future may very well have solved the problems of instability or steady growth or inadequate public investment that trouble us today, but the society that emerges under its new framework will nonetheless be one in which men are still subservient to the economic demands of a market environment.

Nowhere is this apt to pose a more serious problem than along the extended frontier where technology interacts with society. This interaction takes two forms. One, which we may call the *direct effect*, is revealed as the immediate change in the environment brought about by the application of a new technique such as the computerized control of production, or the use of a new product such as jet transport. This effect, as we know from experience, may bring radical changes into economic or social life, but these changes have at least been consciously introduced into society (although often with inadequate appreciation of their immediate impact).

But there is as well an *indirect effect* of technology—an effect that diffuses throughout society as the secondary consequence of new machinery or new processes. Thus the indirect effect of the new technology of automation (whose direct effect is simply to lower costs) is job displacement; the indirect effect of the technology of medicine and health is an aging population; the indirect effect of the technology of war is the creation of a military-industrial economic sector. Not least we find as a general indirect effect of all modern technology an increasing complexity, size, and hierarchical organization of production which gives rise in turn to a growing need for public intervention into and coordination of the economic process itself.

Against this tremendous invasion of technology, a market economy offers but one instrument of control—the profit or loss stemming from the direct effect of the particular technology in question. As to its side effects, the market mechanism proper has no controls whatsoever. As a result, the invasion of technology becomes an essentially disruptive force, continuously upsetting the patterns of life, but in a haphazard rather than a preordained manner.

Admittedly, the regulation of technology must be a matter of the greatest difficulty under any social order. But under a system that abdicates as much decision making as possible to the rule of profit, the possibilities for a rational restraint over the forces rearranging our lives shrinks to a minimum. Whether planned or not, capitalism is essentially defenseless before the revolutionizing impact of its technical drive. Indeed, of all the limits within which capitalism must operate, its essential passivity before the onslaughts of technology is the most unyielding—although, as we shall subsequently see, in its very helpless surrender to technology lies the means by which the limits of the system will eventually be overcome.

Thus planning within capitalism encounters a basic obstacle in its inability to surmount the operative principles by which the market system works. But there is as well a second and no less important barrier to planning that inhibits not only its techniques but its goals. We may call it the limitation of the *capitalist imagination.*

The quality of this imagination is most clearly revealed if we think for a moment of the "visionary" glimpses of the future often spelled out for us by business spokesmen —a future of enormous affluence, technical marvels, and widespread leisure. There is much in these vistas that is genuinely new and rich with possibilities for material betterment. But there is also something inherent in them that remains unmentioned, indeed unnoticed. It is that these imagined societies of the future still depend on "workers," however well off, who work for "businessmen," however enlightened, in a system motivated and directed by the commercial impulse, however tempered or refined. A society in which there were no workers or businessmen as we understand the terms; or in which the categories of privilege or disprivilege had been fundamentally altered; or where the pressures of the marketplace had been replaced by some other means of assuring economic continuity —all these possibilities for the development of human society are absent from the capitalist imagination. More than that, they are dismissed as "utopian."

The consequence is that what is left within the scope of the capitalist imagination is not a social world sufficiently different from our own to serve as a lodestar for the distant future. Albeit unwittingly, this is set forth all too clearly in the peroration of one of the McKinsey lectures by Frederick R. Kappel, President of A.T.&T.:

> We are involved in one of the great ideological struggles of all times. We are in it so deep that it is hard to see it in perspective. But essentially it is a contest between two quite basic concepts. One is that men are capable of faith in ideas that lift their minds and hearts, ideas that raise their sights and give them hope, energy, and enthusiasm. Opposing this is the belief that the pursuit of material ends is all that life on this earth is about.

The words are eloquent enough, but alas, what do they

reveal? Which side, ours or theirs, is the side of "ideas that lift minds and hearts," which the side that believes "the pursuit of material ends is all that life on this earth is about"? In the breath-taking ambiguity of this intended affirmation of business faith, the unseeing confusion of identities meant to be so clearly polarized, lies an all too clear exposition of the weakness that inhabits the very center of the capitalist imagination.

It is not that the ideals of capitalism are necessarily bad. At its best the philosophy of the businessman is sober and decent, matter-of-fact and conserving. The problem rather is that the society it envisages, even at the disappearance point of the horizon of the mind, is essentially the same society, although writ larger, as our own.

We cannot be sure what effect such a constricted view of the future may have on the aspirations and attitudes of most American citizens. It is likely that for the majority who are understandably concerned with their material lot, it would make no difference whatsoever. But for a not unimportant minority—I think of college youth and of the intellectual community—the absence of any transcendent secular goal is apt to present an oppressive limitation to thought and spirit. Indeed, in my opinion the present anarchic mood of youth may well be due to just such a lack of a visionary future to which to bend its hopes and efforts.

☆ 5 ☆

Whatever the ultimate effect of this stiflement at home, there is another area where the limitations of the capitalist imagination are likely to be of very great importance. This is in the contest with communism for the leadership of world opinion and for the guidance of future world society.

It is hardly necessary to speak of the power of communism as a force bearing on American capitalism. Yet in appraising that force we fail to articulate that which is most threatening about it to ourselves as members or protagonists of the capitalist way of life. This is not the expansive nationalism, the aggressive and uncompromising philosophy, the political or military ambitions of the two great Communist societies. It is the presence of communism as a viable social system that has dispensed with our institutions of privilege, and that therefore faces capitalism with the living refutation of their necessity. In a fundamental sense, communism puts capitalism on trial before the bar of history—not with the advantages of a new society claiming the future but with the disadvantages of an old society hanging onto the past.

In this trial it matters not that communism has its own system of privilege, in some ways as primitive as our own. Nor does it count for much that capitalist performance on many fronts is manifestly superior to that of communism. What matters is that communism has demonstrated the mutability and historic transiency of our particular social order, and that that social order can never again feel entirely secure in its claims to permanence and legitimacy.

I believe it is this sense of historic unease that lies behind the deep, uncritical, and often unreasoning hostility of America toward communism. The reasons we cite for our fear and hatred—the undeniable acts of cruelty and repression, of aggression and intolerance, of intrigue and untrustworthiness, can be duplicated in many non-Communist countries—in Portugal, in Spain, in the Union of South Africa, in various Latin-American dictatorships past and present. There, however, they have never roused in us the fervor or revulsion they do when discovered in the Communist world. In part this is no doubt because these other nations are small and weak and do not constitute centers of national power comparable to Russia or China (although hardly Cuba); in part because they do not seek to export their particular world views. But more deeply, especially among the conservative interests of this country, I think it is because the existence of communism frightens American capitalism as the existence of Protestantism once frightened the Catholic Church, or the French Revolution the English aristocracy.

This fundamental threat of communism is not likely to decline over the next generation. Rather, it is apt to grow. In Russia, the prospect is clearly for substantial economic expansion, although probably not at the rates of the past; for the gradual improvement of the still dreary life of its people; for a continuation of its impressive scientific advances; for further intellectual and perhaps political liberalization. For China no such sanguine assurances can be given, but by comparison with the situation in India, where economic collapse and political dismemberment are all too dishearteningly possible, its continuing emergence as the unquestioned leader of Asia seems hardly likely to be reversed. In Latin America and Africa the outlook can only be for political turmoil as the aspirations of excited masses outdistance any conceivable pace of progress, certainly that available under their present inept and often reactionary leadership. In the ensuing unrest, radical leaders are bound to emerge, and it would be a miracle if they were not inclined, to some degree, toward communism or some kind of national collectivism.

This tendency is liked to be reinforced by the very ideological limitations of capitalism we have been concerned with. If we look to the developing nations, now thrashing about in the quicksands of development, we find in nearly all of them a yearning not alone for material progress but for a great social and political, even spiritual, transformation. However millennial these hopes, however certain to be dashed, they are not to be lightly disregarded.

The leaders and elites of the young nations, like those of our own youth, are looking for a model of a society that will fire them to great efforts, and it is unlikely that they will find this model—at least so far as its economic structure is concerned—in the market-based and wealth-protecting philosophy of capitalism.

All these considerations point to the very great likelihood that communism or radical national collectivism will make substantial inroads during the coming generation or two, perhaps by conquest or subversion, but more probably by the decay of existing orders unable to handle the terrible demands of political awakening and economic reformation. On the other side of the world balance sheet, it is far from hopeful that American capitalism will add many names to its side of the book. A few nations, mainly in Latin America, may develop into full-fledged capitalist economies, but the great majority of the underdeveloped world, although envying the material success of capitalism, is not likely to be attracted in its direction.

Given this grave outlook, what would be its impact on America?

We have already witnessed the initial impact in the substantial militarization of American capitalism. The so-called military-industrial complex (to which should be added "political" as an equal partner) today contributes between 8 and 10 percent to the Gross National Product—a percentage roughly half again as large as the share of all government spending within the economy in World War I. In the 1960's military expenditure has regularly exceeded the sum total of all personal income taxes, has accounted for one-fourth of all federal public works, has directly employed some 3.2 million workers in defense industries and another 1.1 million as civilian employees of the Defense Department and the services; has provided 30 percent of all manufacturing jobs in Kansas, 28 percent in the state of Washington, over 20 percent in another five states, and between 8 and 10 percent in seven more; has subsidized about one third of all research in the United States; and not least, has come to be accepted as a normal and permanent fixture of American economic, social, and political life by all groups including not least the academic. No attempt to speak of the long-run prospects for American capitalism can overlook the central fact that it is now a semimilitarized economy and that it will very probably become even more so during the next decade.

In this dangerous situation it is important for us to try to clarify the specific influence over the direction of events that can be ascribed to capitalism proper—which is to say, to the business interest in society. According to Marxism— or, more properly, Leninism—the business structure itself inherently presses the state toward armed conflict. Lenin's theory of imperialism maintains that capitalist firms must reach overseas for sources of cheap supply or for new markets, and that where trade goes the flag follows. Then, as rival national economic interests collide or (in the modernized version of the theory) as the interests of imperialist firms come into conflict with those of colonialists, national force must be used to ensure economic domination.

The fierce economic conflicts of capitalist nations prior to World War II, the long history of capitalist suppression of colonials continuing down to the present in some parts of Africa, the huge and jealously guarded interests of the United States and other capitalist nations in the oil regions of the Near East or Latin America, all make it impossible to dismiss the notion of a belligerent capitalist imperialism as mere fiction. At the same time, it does not follow that capitalism is intrinsically war-producing just because it has been the cause of international friction in the past. Even a cursory review of the nations initiating aggressive actions since 1945—North Korea, India, China, Israel, Britain, France, Russia, Indonesia, the United States—should raise doubts as to the exclusive capitalist predisposition to war. More important, an analysis of the roots of belligerency in the more warlike capitalisms, specifically prewar Germany or Japan, must emphasize the leading role played by purely military or lingering feudal elements, and the largely passive, although certainly not always reluctant, part taken by capitalist groups.

On somewhat more Marxian lines, Victor Perlo has made a determination of the direct economic interest of the top American corporations in war or peace by calculating the degree to which each would benefit by disarmament via lower taxes, or lose from it because of reduced defense business. He concludes that the economic self-interest of the biggest corporations is more or less evenly divided, with half profiting from a defense economy and half—including such giants as General Motors and U.S. Steel—being penalized by it. Assuming that big businessmen would be motivated to oppose or support disarmament from such motives, it is at least reassuring to note that nothing like a monolithic "pro-war" economic interest can be said to prevail within American capitalism.

Further, the imperialist thrust that increased both the chances and the causes of war in the late nineteenth century seems to be giving way to less dangerous forms of international relationship. Property interests that once had to be defended by force of arms are now protected by government insurance, so that the threat of expropriation can be viewed with greater equanimity than in the past. International relationships that formerly allowed large capitalist enterprises to intervene directly into the economic and political life of colonial nations have been succeeded by relationships in which the independence of action of foreign companies is severely restricted. The laissez-faire markets of the world are slowly yielding to controlled marketing arrangements. In a word, the politics of nationalism has asserted its pre-eminence over the economics of imperialism, with the salutary consequence of a diminution in the role of business as the active initiator of foreign economic policy.

Thus, the role of capitalism proper in the struggle for

world power does not give undue cause for anxiety. Although there are capitalist elements who fan or support an aggressive foreign policy, the main body of business sentiment can hardly be described as warlike. Unfortunately, that does not mean the chances for conflict are therefore small. To repeat again a cardinal point of these essays, business is not the only power center within capitalist societies, and in America the military and the civil branches of government contain more than their share of belligerent-minded leaders who are in a position to influence foreign policy. Then, too, given the strength of the generalized hatred of communism among the lower and middle classes, any sentiment for aggressive measures against "the Reds" is not apt to lack for followers.

In this situation, given the reciprocal posture of the other side, it is difficult to see how a major conflict could be avoided, were not the consequences of all-out warfare so terrifying. On both sides, Communist as well as capitalist, the drive of ideological fervor and the desire to validate a position in history press toward a "final" solution, and only the instinct of self-preservation—fortunately the single most powerful instinct—holds back the military-minded, the fundamentalist, the ambitious, or simply the self-righteous. As a result, the most probable outlook becomes a continuation of the military-political struggle on the scale of Korea or Vietnam, where both sides must exert efforts to keep the degree of involvement, in terms of men and prestige, below the flash point of uncontrollable conflict.

The danger is that a succession of such involvements, most of them probably ending uphappily or with doubtful victories, may encourage the rise of a strict garrison state, marked by an atmosphere of internal repression and external belligerence. This grave possibility may well be the single most dangerous eventuality during the next decade or two when the chances for Communist "take-overs" will be greatest. But the longer-term future is far from foreclosed along such lines. On both sides of the great divide, forces are at work that can lessen the intensity of the conflict. One of these is the enhanced prospect for international stabilization, once the worst is over and those nations that are going to go Communist or national-collectivist have done so. A second hopeful possibility is the growth of a greater degree of isolationism in American politics—or perhaps one should say a lesser degree of interventionism—compounded in part of disillusion, in part of fear, and in part of a more realistic appreciation of our inability to affect the unruly tides of world history. Yet another force for peaceful accomodation is that the specter of Communist "world domination" will be dispelled by the sight of Communist nations in intense rivalry, just as the Communist world may be relieved by the continuing evidence of intercapitalist frictions.

And, finally, we can hope that within a generation or so new concerns posed by enormous world populations; interlocked global technical devices for communications, transport, power, and other uses; vanishing fossil fuel supplies;

and a worldwide polluted atmosphere will cause the present ideological fervor to subside under more pressing problems, just as did the great religious animosities of the past.

Not all the preconditions for such a turn of events lie in our own hands. Much depends on the continuation of the present trend toward the fragmentation and gradual liberalization of the Communist world. But, given this opportunity, there seems at least a reasonable chance that American and European capitalism can find a *modus vivendi* with the other side. Here once again the critical determination of direction is apt to reside with the new ideology and the new elites rising within capitalism. Indeed, if there are limits to the adaptability of capitalism before the untoward development of world events, these limits appear to reside, more than is the case with the other challenges before the system, in the quality of the "new men" who are rising to power within it.

☆   6   ☆

It is time to revert to the question we set ourselves at the end of our initial essay. There we asserted that America was still a nation largely bound by the business ideology— that is, limited in its programs, policies, and ideas to those ventures that were compatible with and acceptable to the general consensus of business thought. Even though it seemed clear that nonbusiness elites were steadily moving into positions of greater power at the expense of business executives themselves, these new elites had no vision to offer society, nor any particular destination for it other than that of "capitalism." Thus the definition of "capitalism" seemed of primary importance in establishing the boundaries of change, and for this reason the slow leftward movement of the business ideology assumed a putative central role in enlarging the perimeter of social action.

Nonetheless, at the conclusion of our first essay, a final problem remained. Assuming that the ideology of business would continue along its gradual path of liberalization, how far did this mean that capitalism could change? What limits, we asked, were inherent in the system, rather than in any particularly ideology of the day?

The answer at which we have arrived is necessarily imprecise, but it does not seem entirely indeterminate. In the dynamic process of social change, the economic relationships that give rise to privilege are those that fix the degree of social resistance, and these relationships give us a general indication of what is possible and what is not.

It is not difficult to recapitulate this difference. What seems possible is to bring about social change—in the distribution of wealth or in the control over output or in the imaginative destination of society or its relations with the noncapitalist world—that stops short of an intolerable curtailment of those privileges that all elites within American capitalism—and indeed, the general public as well—are eager to protect. What is impossible, within the time period in which we are interested, is to effect changes that would involve the virtual destruction of the central institutions of the system itself. This means, for example, that the distribution of wealth can be corrected at the bottom but not at the top. It means that the control over output can be improved very greatly, but that the essential commercial character of a market system is beyond alteration. It means that a considerable accommodation can be made with the noncapitalist world, but that the imagination of that world (or of the American mind) is not likely to be captured by the capitalist rhetoric. There are, in a word, deep-seated attributes to the quality of American life that constitute an impregnable inner keep of the system of American capitalism as we know it.

And yet, if we now recall our earlier concern with feudalism, we will recall that, despite the seeming impregnability of its institutions in the thirteenth century, by the eighteenth century somehow the system had nonetheless changed out of all recognition. Hence we must ask whether the inner keep of capitalism, although out of range of bombardment today, may not also be ultimately vulnerable to the kind of penetration that finally invested the feudal citadels of privilege.

The question asks us to reflect on how feudalism expired. The answer is not by revolution. However important for other reasons, the revolutions of the eighteenth and nineteenth centuries merely ripped off the tattered covers of feudalism to reveal new economic societies, already full-formed and operative, beneath them. Rather, feudalism gave way to capitalism as part of a subversive process of historic change in which a newly emerging attribute of daily life proved to be as irresistibly attractive to the privileged orders of feudalism as it was ultimately destructive of them.

This subversive influence was the gradual infiltration of commercial relationships and cash exchanges into the everyday round of feudal existence, each act of marketing binding men more fully into the cash nexus and weakening by that degree the traditional duties and relationships on which feudalism was based. Against this progressive monetization the old order struggled in vain, for the temptations and pleasures of the cash economy were greater than the erosion of privileges that went with it: "It is the costliness of clothes that is destroying the nobles of our German lands," wrote one chronicler, telling of a widow who sold a village to raise the price of a blue velvet gown to wear to a tournament.

Could there be an equivalent of that powerfully disintegrative and yet constitutive force in our day—a force sufficiently overwhelming to render impotent the citadel of capitalism and yet as irresistibly attractive to its masters as the earlier current of change was to feudalism? I think there is such a force, and that it already bulks very large within our world, where it is cumulatively and irreversibly altering the social system even more rapidly than did the process of monetization during the medieval era. This revolutionary power is the veritable explosion of organized knowledge and its applied counterpart, scientific technology, in modern times.

The extraordinary rate of expansion of this explosion is sufficiently familiar to require only a word of exposition. There is, for instance, the often-quoted but still astonishing statement that of all the scientists who have ever lived in all of history, half are alive today. There is the equally startling calculation that the volume of scientific publication during the past ten to fifteen years is as large as or larger than that of all previous ages. Such examples are no doubt more impressionistic than exact, but they serve accurately enough to convey the notion of the exponential growth of scientific inquiry in our day. As to the equally phenomenal growth of the powers of the technology, if that needs any demonstration, there is the contrast cited by Kenneth Boulding between the decades needed to reconstruct Germany after the Thirty Years' War or the centuries needed to recuperate from the physical destruction that accompanied the collapse of the Roman Empire and the scant twenty years in which the shattered and burned cities of modern Europe and Japan were rebuilt after the Second World War.

This explosion of science and scientifically based technology is often thought of as a product *of* capitalism, in so

far as it arose within a capitalist milieu and in an age dominated by capitalism. Yet the association was far more one
of coexistence than of causal interrelation. Science, as we
know it, began well before capitalism existed and did not
experience its full growth until well after capitalism was
solidly entrenched. At best we can say that the secular air
of bourgeois culture was compatible with, perhaps even
conducive to, scientific investigation, but we can hardly
credit the acceleration of scientific activities after the
middle of the nineteenth century—the work of Darwin,
Maxwell, Rutherford, Freud, Mendel, not to mention the
great contemporary mathematicians—to the direct stimulus
or patronage of capitalism itself.

Perhaps more surprising, even scientific technology ex-
hibits but little debt to the existence of capitalism. The
technology on which capitalism began its long course of
growth in the eighteenth and early nineteenth centuries
was mainly of a pragmatic, intuitive, prescientific kind.
The Second Law of Thermodynamics was not formulated
by Kelvin until 1851, and its immense practical significance
was only slowly realized thereafter. The English textile,
iron and steel, or chemical industries were founded and
prospered with no "scientific" underpinnings at all. The
same is true for the young railroad industry, for canal
building, or road laying. Even as late as the mid-nineteenth
century, a proposal by the famous Siemens brothers of
Berlin that cable be scientifically tested before being laid
was dismissed by British engineers as "humbug."

There was, of course, a certain amount of systematic industrial experimentation in the mid-1800's, and a burst of important inventions, many of which depended on some application of scientific knowledge, in the second half of the century. Yet the deliberate employment of scientific investigation to create or refine the technology of production was considerably delayed in arriving. In this country the first private industrial laboratory was not built until 1900 by the General Electric Company, and organized research and development on a large scale did not really get under way until 1913.

Thus we find the flowering of science and the application of science to technology—the very hallmarks of the modern era—to be currents that arose *within* capitalism, but that do not owe their existence directly to capitalism. Rather, like the first manifestations of the market in the medieval era, science and its technology emerge as a great underground river whose tortuous course has finally reached the surface during the age of capitalism, but which springs from far distant sources. But that is not where the resemblance ends. As with the emergent market forces, the river of scientific change, having now surfaced, must cut its own channel through the existing social landscape—channel that will, as in the case with the money orientation in medieval life, profoundly alter the nature of the existing terrain. Indeed, if we ask what force in our day might in time be strong enough to undercut the bastions of privilege and function of capitalism and to create its own institutions and social structures in their place, the answer must surely be the one force that dominates our age—the power of science and of scientific technology.

There is, I suspect, little to argue about as to the commanding presence of science in modern times. What is likely to be a good deal less readily accepted, however, is the contention that this force will cause drastic modifications in, or even the eventual supersession of, capitalism. For at first glance the new current of history seems to have imparted an immense momentum to capitalism by providing it with the very thing it most required—a virtually inexhaustible source of invention and innovation to ensure its economic growth. Merely to review in our minds the broad areas of investment and economic output that owe their existence entirely to the laboratory work of the past three decades—the nuclear and space establishments, electronics, the computerization of industry, the wonder drugs, the creation of new materials such as plastics—is to reveal the breadth of this new gulf stream of economic nourishment.

Yet, like the attractions of the cash market for the feudal lord, the near-term advantages of science and technology conceal long-term conflicts and incompatibilities between this new force of history and its host society. Just as the insertion of cash exchanges into the fine structure of feudalism ultimately made obsolete the functional mechanism of a manorial society, so the insinuation of science and technology into the interstices of business enterprise promises to outmode the fundamental working arrangements of capitalism.

At least one of these disruptive manifestations is already familiar to us. This is the tendency of technology to create social problems that require *non-market controls* to correct or forestall. In part these agencies of control are contained and concealed within the centers of production themselves, where they show up as the rising echelons of corporate administration and supervision that are needed to regulate the underlying traffic of production. In part the controls show up in the familiar bureaus of government that directly oversee the operation of the new technology—the bureaus that cope, with greater or lesser success, with the social repercussions of transportation, nuclear energy, drugs, air pollution, etc. In still a different aspect, the controls invade areas of social life rather than production, as in the astonishing network of government required solely to manage the automobile (an effort that requires the labor of one out of every ten persons employed by all state and local goverments), or in the multiplying administrative requirements of the mega-city, itself so much a product of modern technology. Meanwhile, in the background of the social system the controls are manifest as the growing apparatus of regulation over wages and prices, and over the total flow of economic activity all ultimately traceable to the need to intervene more closely into an economy of increasing technological complexity.

Not that the disruptive effect of technology is itself a

new phenomenon. The dislocations of the technology of the prescientific age—say the spinning jenny—were quite as great as those of the modern age, such as the computer. The difference is that in an earlier age the repair of technological disturbances was largely consigned to the adaptive powers of the individual, to the ameliorative efforts of small-scale local government, and to the annealing powers of the market itself. Today, however, these traditional agencies of social recovery can no longer cope effectively with the entrance of technology. The individual, now typically a member of a small urban family rather than of a large extended rural family, is much less capable of withstanding economic displacement without external assistance. The local community, faced with large scale problems of unemployment or ecological maladjustment brought about by technical change, has no recourse but to turn to the financial help and expertise available only from larger government units. The market, which no longer "clears" when the marketers are enormous firms rather than atomistic business units, also discovers that the only antidote to grave economic disjunction is the countervailing influence or *force majeur* of central governing authority. In a word, technology in the modern era seems to be exerting a steady push from many levels and areas of the economy in the direction of a society of *organization.*

This well-known effect of technical progress is, however, only the most obvious, and perhaps not the most fundamental, way in which the scientific current works against the enveloping economic order. A deeper cutting edge of technology lies in another attribute of its impact on society —its capacity to render redundant the physical energies of man, at least as these energies are mainly harnessed in a market setting. That is, machines do man's work for him, thereby freeing him from the bonds of toil and, not less important in the context of our inquiry, from the hegemony of the market process.

We can see this disemployment effect most dramatically in the case of agriculture. A century ago farming, as the basic activity of society, absorbed the working energies of 60 to 70 percent of the population. Today, although no less essential to the provisioning of the human community, agriculture requires only the effort of some 8 percent of the population (working only two thirds as long as its forebears in the 1860's) and even this small fraction will probably be further reduced to about 4 to 5 percent within a decade.

But equally startling is the labor-displacing effect of modern technology in that congeries of activities associated with the extraction of basic materials from nature and their fabrication, assembly, conversion, or transport to point of sale. If we look back to 1900 we find that about 38 of every 100 working Americans were then employed in mining, manufacturing, the generation of power, transport, or construction. Since then science and technology have given us a stupendous array of new products, each requiring large amounts of human effort—the automobile and truck, the whole range of consumer durables, the communications industry, office machinery, new metals, fabrics, and materials of all kinds to name but a few. Yet at the end of that period the total requirements for labor in all the goods-centered industries had risen by only *two percentage points*, to 40 out of every 100 workers. As fast as demand grew for these myriad products, that fast did technology and science permit labor to be economized. During the era of the greatest increase in factory production ever known, virtually no increase in labor was needed—indeed, since the hours of work fell, there was actually a relatively *decreased* need for human effort in the output of goods.

The point is important enough to warrant another word of exposition. What technology has done over a fifty year span is to enable relatively fewer workers in the "goods sector" to supply the needs of a richer population. As the table below shows, this is due to a deep penetration of technology into mining, construction, transportation, and utilities. In manufacturing proper there was a 12 percent increase in labor needs in terms of relative *numbers* of men, although in terms of *hours*, there was a reduction of labor requirements here too. By way of contrast, there has been an increase in the proportion of workers required to provide services—retail and wholesale trade, finance, government, domestic service, etc.

This secular shift takes on new significance in the light of the technology of automation. We do not yet know whether the new devices that count, sort, remember,

check, and respond to stimuli will intensify the labor displacement process in those industries where technology has
already long been at work. But there is reason to believe
that technology has begun to invade what has heretofore
been a sanctuary of relatively unmechanized work—the
vast numbers of jobs in the office, administrative, and serv-

WORKERS PER 1,000 POPULATION, UNITED STATES

	1900	1965
Mining	10	3
Manufacturing	82	92
Construction	22	16
Transportation and utilities	27	21
All "goods sector" (above)	141	132
All service sector	93	178

SOURCE: For 1900, *Historical Statistics of the United States,* Bureau of
the Census, Washington, 1960, Series D 57–71; for 1965, *Economic Indicators.*

ice occupations. In 1900 less than one fourth of the total
working population was employed in these nonfarm, non-
factory kinds of work—as lawyers, teachers, government
officials, stenographers, bookkeepers, clerks, servants. By
1960 more than half the labor force was in these jobs. And
now, into this varied group of occupations, technology is
starting to penetrate in the form of machines as complex as
those that can read and sort checks or as relatively simple
as those that dispense coffee and sandwiches.

This is not to maintain that no new areas of employment

exist to take the place of those occupied by machinery. Certainly there remain very large and still untapped possibilities for work in the repair and reconstruction of the cities; the provision of education, public safety, and conveyance; in the improvement of health and recreation facilities; in the counseling of the young and the care of the aged; in the beautification of the environment. Provided only that demand can be marshaled for these activities, there will surely be no dearth of job prospects for the coming generation.

But that is precisely the point. The incursion of technology has pushed the frontiers of work from the farm to the factory, then from the factory to the store and the office, and now from store and office into a spectrum of jobs whose common denominator is that they require *public action and public funds* for their initiation and support. The employment-upsetting characteristics of technology thus act to speed capitalism along the general path of planning and control down which it is simultaneously impelled by the direct environment-upsetting impact of technological change.

If we look further ahead, the necessity for planning is apt to become still more pressing. Given the trajectory of present scientific capabilities, the day of a "fully automated" society is by no means a fantasy, although its realization may well require another century, or possibly more. But in the long evolutionary perspective in which we are now interested, one can surely look to the time when all or nearly all of the paid labor of our present society outside the categories of professional or managerial work (and a good deal within those echelons) could be accomplished by machinery with but little human supervision. That is to say, we can, without too much difficulty, imagine a time when as small a proportion of the labor force as now suffices to overprovide us with food will serve to turn out the manufactured staples, the houses, the transportation, the retail services, even the governmental supervision that will be required.

What the leisured—not to use the word "unemployed" —fraction of the population will then do with itself is an interesting and important question. If it is not to starve, it must be given the chance to share in society's output. Should there exist sufficient modes of activity resistive to mechanization, this may be accomplished through the market mechanism: instead of taking in one another's wash, we will buy one another's paintings. But even in this best outcome, the underlying processes of production, now enormously mechanized and intricately interconnected, would almost certainly require some form of coordination other than the play of market forces. And then, of course, if the leisured population does not find adequate opportunities for unmechanizable employments, it will simply have to be given a right to share in society's output—an even more basic infringement on the hegemony of the market.

Thus, in a manner not entirely dissimilar from the way in which the steady monetization of feudal life weakened the relevance and effectiveness of manorial ties, the incorporation of technology into the working mechanism of the capitalist system also renders less relevant and effective the market ties on which that system is ultimately founded. Partly because of the social disturbances it creates in an urban industrial environment, partly because of the progressive compression of the need for human effort in the provisioning of society, the steady entrance of technology into capitalism forces new social structures of control and supervision to rise within and over the marketplace.

But the erosion of the market goes deeper yet. For the introduction of technology has one last effect whose ultimate implications for the metamorphosis of capitalism are perhaps greatest of all. This is the effect of technology in steadily raising the average level of well-being, thereby gradually bringing to an end the condition of material need as an effective stimulus for human behavior.

This is by all odds the most generally hailed attribute of science and technology, for everyone recognizes that the end to want would represent the passage over an historic watershed. But it must be equally clear that such a passage will also represent a basic revision of the existential situation that has hitherto provided the main impetus for work. As the level of average enjoyments increases, as needs diminish and wants become of such relative unimportance that they can be easily foregone, the traditional stimuli of capitalism begin to lose their force. Occupations now become valued for their instrinic pleasures rather than for their extrinsic rewards. The very decision to work or not becomes a matter of personal preference rather than of economic necessity. More telling, the drive for profit—the nuclear core of capitalist energy—becomes blunted as the purchasable distinctions of wealth decline. In a society of the imaginable wealth implicit in another hundred years of technical progress, who will wish to be the rich man's servant at any price? In such a society the services that have always been the prerogative of the rich will have to be performed by machine or dispensed with altogether—a state of affairs already visible in many areas if we compare the life of the wealthy today with that of the past.

All this is no doubt a gain in human dignity, as the bowers and scrapers, the waiters and flunkeys—not to mention the performers of menial tasks everywhere—escape from work hitherto performed only under the lash of necessity. But that is not an end to it. As a result of this inestimable gain in personal freedom, a fundamental assurance for social viability also vanishes, for the market stimuli that bring about social provisioning are no longer met with obedient responses. One has but to imagine employees in an industry of central importance going on strike, not with the slim backing of unemployment insurance and a small union supplement, as today, but with liquid assets sufficient to maintain them, if need be, for a year or more, to envisage the potential for social disorder inherent in the attainment of a genuinely widespread and substantial affluence.

Yet it is precisely such an affluence that is within clear sight provided that the impetus of science and technology continues to propel the economy for another century. In this impasse there is but one possible solution. *Some authority other than the market must be entrusted with the allocation of men to the essential posts of society should they lack for applicants.*

We have concerned ourselves so far only with the curious two-edged effect of science and technology on the functional aspects of capitalism, both sustaining and hurrying along its growth, and by that very fact pressing it into a more organized social form. Now we must pay heed to a second and perhaps even more critical effect. This is the conquest of the capitalist imagination by science and scientific technology.

I think it is fair to say that capitalism as an *idea* has never garnered much enthusiasm. The acquisitive behavior on which it is perforce based has suffered all through history from the moral ambivalence in which it has been held; all efforts to raise money-making to the level of a positive virtue have failed. The self-interest of the butcher and the baker to whom Adam Smith appealed in lieu of their benevolence may serve as powerful sources of social energy, but not as powerful avatars of the social imagination.

By way of contrast, I think it is also fair to say that

science and its technical application *is* the burning idea of
the twentieth century, comparable in its impact on men's
minds to the flush of the democratic enthusiasm of the late
eighteenth century or to the political commitment won by
communism in the early twentieth. The altruism of science,
its "purity," the awesome vistas it opens, and the venerable
path it has followed, have won from all groups, and especially from the young, exactly that passionate interest and
conviction that is so egregiously lacking to capitalism as a
way of life.

And it is not only within capitalism that the charismatic
powers of science reveal their extraordinary appeal. Within
the citadel of economic commitment itself, inside Russia,
we hear that science, and science alone, has the capacity to
penetrate and to overrule the orthodoxies of Marxist philosophy. A. J. Ayer, after lecturing at the Faculty of Philosophy in Moscow University in 1962 reports: "The prestige of science is so great that it is now becoming a question
of [the philosophers] having to adapt their philosophical
principles to current scientific theory than the other way
round."

It is not alone that science carries a near-religious ethos
of conviction and even sacrifice. In Russia as well as in
America the new elites arising within the framework of the
old society—and as a social order focused on economics,
contemporary communism is, like capitalism, an "old"
society—owe their ascendancy and their allegiance in large
part to science. The scientific cadres proper, the social sci-

entists, the government administrative personnel, even the military, all look to science not merely as the vehicle of their expertise but as the magnetic north of their compass of values. These new elites, as we have indicated, have not as yet divorced their social goals from those of the society to which they are still glad to pay allegiance, and no more than the thirteenth-century merchants huddled under the walls of a castle do they see themselves as the potential architects and lords of a society built around their own functions. But, as with the merchants, we can expect that such notions will in time emerge and assert their primacy over the aims of the existing order.

What sorts of notions are these apt to be?

One general direction of thought will surely be the primacy of scientific discovery as a central purpose of society, a *raison d'être* for its existence, perhaps even a vehicle for its religious impulses. To partake in the adventure of the scientific mission or its technological realization should accordingly become as dominating a motivation for the future as the wish to participate in economic adventure is at present, and no doubt the distribution of social resources and of privileges will reflect this basic orientation toward scientific exploration and application.

Not less characteristic will be an emphasis on rational solutions to social problems that are today not yet subject to human direction. Not alone economic affairs (which should become of secondary importance), but the numbers and location of the population, its genetic quality, the manner of social domestication of children, the choice of lifework—even the very duration of life itself—are all apt to become subjects for scientific investigation and control. Indeed, the key word of the new society is apt to be *control*.

It is tempting but idle to venture beyond these few suggestions. What manner of life, what institutions, what ideologies may serve the purposes of a society dedicated to the accumulation of scientific knowledge and power we cannot foretell; the variations may well be as great as those observable in societies dedicated to the accumulation of material wealth. Nor does there seem to be much point in attempting to foresee by what precise stratagems the elites and ideas of the future may finally assert their claims. Who, for instance, could have foreseen that the long evolution into capitalism would require not merely the diffusion of market relations but the indispensable way station of mercantilism, the "mixed economy" of the eighteenth century? Or who could have predicted that the nobility of England, traditionally one of the haughtiest in Europe, would learn to protect its social privileges by intermarrying with the despised mercantile families, so that English feudalism could melt imperceptibly into a capitalist aristocracy, whereas in France the nobility would widen the social distance from the bourgeoisie until, as de Tocqueville says, "the two classes were not merely rivals, they were foes"?

Such twists of the historic route warn us that historic projection is rarely, if ever, a matter of simple extrapolation from the present and recent past. Neither routes nor time-tables are laid out in history with an eye to regularity or a concern for Euclidean simplicities. Should there arise radical parties in America, broadly based and aimed at a rational reorganization of economic affairs, the pace of transition would be quicker. Should there not—the perhaps pessimistic premise on which this analysis is based, for I do not believe that such parties are a likely phenomenon if capitalism achieves the degree of change that is within its compass—change will still occur, but more slowly. Veblen was too impatient for his engineers to take over; Schumpeter more realistic when he advised the intelligentsia to be prepared to wait in the wings for possibly a century, a "short run" in affairs of this kind, he said.

So, too, the examples of the past discourage us from attempting to prophesy the manner of demise of the social order to be superseded. The new institutions of social and economic control will appear only slowly and sporadically amid the older forms, and will lack for some time an articulate conception of a purposively constituted and consciously directed social system. The old ideas of the proper primacy of economic aims will linger together with newer ideas of the priority of scientific interests. And no doubt the privileges of the older order will endure side by side with those of the new, just as titles of nobility exist to this very day, some assimilated to the realities of capitalism, some adorning doormen or taxi drivers. It is conceivable that violence may attend the displacement of power and responsibility from one elite to another, but more probably the transfer will be imperceptible; managed, as in the case of the English aristocracy, by the sons of the old elite entering the professions of the new.

All these are the merest speculations, difficult to avoid entirely, not to be taken too literally. What is certain is only one thing. It is the profound incompatibility between the new idea of the active use of science within society and the idea of capitalism as a social system.

The conflict does not lie on the surface, in any clash between the immediate needs of science and those of capitalism. It lies in the ideas that ultimately inform both worlds. The world of science, as it is applied by society, is committed to the idea of man as a being who shapes his collective destiny; the world of capitalism to an idea of man as one who permits his common social destination to take care of itself. The essential idea of a society built on scientific engineering is to impose human will on the social universe; that of capitalism to allow the social universe to unfold as if it were beyond human interference.

Before the activist philosophy of science as a social instrument, this inherent social passivity of capitalism becomes archaic and eventually intolerable. The "self-regulating" economy that is its highest social achievement stands condemned by its absence of a directing intelligence, and each small step taken to correct its deficiencies only advertises the inhibitions placed on the potential exercise of purposeful thought and action by its remaining barriers of ideology and privilege. In the end capitalism is weighed in the scale of science and found wanting, not alone as a system but as a philosophy.

That an ascendant science, impatient to substitute reason for blind obedience, inquiry for ideology, represents a great step forward for mankind I do not doubt. Yet it seems necessary to end on a cautionary note. Just as the prescient medievalist might have foreseen in capitalism the possibilities for the deformation of human life as well as for its immense improvement, so the approaching world of scientific predominance has its darker as well as its more luminous side. Needless to say, there lurks a dangerous collectivist tinge in the prospect of controls designed for the enlargement of man but inherently capable of his confinement as well. But beyond that there is, in the vista of a scientific quest grimly pursued for its own sake, a chilling reminder of a world where economic gains are relentlessly pursued for their own sake. Science is a majestic driving force from which to draw social energy and inspiration, but its very impersonality, its "value-free" criteria, may make its tutelary elites as remote and unconcerned as the principles in whose name they govern.

Against these cold and depersonalizing possibilities of a scientifically organized world, humanity will have to struggle in the future, as it has had to contend against not dissimilar excesses of economic involvement in this painful— but also liberating—stage of human development. Thus if the dawn of an age of science opens larger possibilities for mankind than it has enjoyed heretofore, it does not yet promise a society whose overriding aim will be the cultivation and enrichment of all human beings, in all their diversity, complexity, and profundity. That is the struggle for the very distant future, which must be begun, nonetheless, today.

NOTES

PAGE 9 One-fifth to almost one-third. S. M. Lipset and R. Bendix, *Social Mobility in Industrial Society* (Berkeley: University of California Press, 1960), p. 178.

10 Size distribution of business and corporations. *U. S. Statistical Abstract* (Washington, 1965), p. 489.

11 Billion-dollar companies. *The Fortune Directory* (New York: Time, Inc., 1965).

15 Berle Projection. *The Modern Corporation and Private Property* (New York: Commerce Clearing House, 1932), p. 44.

15 Top 100 industrials. A. D. H. Kaplan, *Big Enterprise in a Competitive System* (Washington: Brookings Institution, 1964), p. 120.

16 Value added. *Concentration Ratios in American Manufacturing*, Report of Census Bureau to Senate Subcommittee on Anti-Trust and Monopoly, 1963.

16 Victor Fuchs, *The Public Interest*, No. 2, Winter, 1966, pp. 9-10.

16 Adelman, "The Measure of Industrial Concentration," *Review of Economics and Statistics* (November, 1951), p. 295. See also E. S. Mason, *Economic Concentrations and the Monopoly Problem* (New York: Atheneum Publishers [paperback], 1964), pp. 36-44.

137

PAGE 19   471 firms. *U. S. Statistical Abstract* (cited above), p. 504.

19   J. Fred Weston, *The Role of Mergers in the Growth of Large Firms* (Berkeley: University of California Press, 1953).

19   50 largest industrial firms in 1909. Kaplan, *Big Enterprise*, pp. 140-153.

21   Dropout among firms. N. R. Collins and L. E. Preston, "The Size Structure of Industrial Firms," *American Economic Review* (December, 1961), pp. 986-1011.

22   Adelman, "Measure of Industrial Concentration," p. 286.

22   1,000 product classes. Kaplan, *Big Enterprise*, p. 89.

25   Don Villarejo, "Stock Ownership and the Control of Corporations," *New University Thought II* (Autumn, 1961, and Winter, 1962).

25   Gabriel Kolko, *Wealth and Power in America* (New York: Frederick A. Praeger, Inc., 1962), pp. 61-62.

27   Scientific American, *The Big Business Executive*, (New York: The Scientific American, 1965). See also Jay Gould, *The Technical Elite* (New York: Augustus Kelley, 1966), pp. 160-171.

27   M. Newcomer, *The Big Business Executive* (New York: Columbia University Press, 1955), p. 63.

28   Paul A. Baran, *Monthly Review*, July-August, 1962, p. 146.

29   "Official" positions. See Francis X. Sutton, *et al.*, *The American Business Creed* (Cambridge, Mass.: Harvard University Press, 1956). J. W. Prothro, *Dollar Decade* (Baton Rouge: Louisiana State University Press, 1954); K. Schriftgeisser, *Business Comes of Age* (New York: Harper & Row, Publishers, Incorporated, 1960). Also, Heilbroner, "The View from the Top," in *The Business Establishment* (New York: John Wiley & Sons, Inc., 1964).

30   Ralph J. Cordiner, *New Frontiers for Professional Managers* (New York: McGraw-Hill Book Company, 1956), pp. vi-vii.

PAGE 30   McKinsey Lectures. Cordiner, *New Frontiers;* C. Greene-
walt, *The Uncommon Man* (New York: McGraw-Hill
Book Company, 1959); R. Blough, *Free Man and the
Corporation* (New York: McGraw-Hill, 1959); T. V.
Houser, *Big Business and Human Values* (New York:
McGraw-Hill, 1957); F. Kappel, *Vitality in a Business
Enterprise* (New York: McGraw-Hill, 1960); T. Wat-
son, *A Business and Its Beliefs* (New York: McGraw-
Hill, 1963). Not included are subsequent volumes by
Marion Folsom and David Rockefeller.

31   Cordiner, *New Frontiers,* p. 1.

31-32   Houser, *Big Business,* p. ix.

32   Blough, *Free Man,* p. 15; Cordiner, pp. 2-3.

32-33   Watson, *A Business,* p. 80; Cordiner, pp. 19-20.

34   Watson, pp. 87-90.

35   Fortune, *U.S.A., The Permanent Revolution* (Englewood
Cliffs, N.J.: Prentice Hall, 1951), p. 80.

36   Western Electric. J. Duscha, *Arms, Money and Politics*
(New York: Ives Washburn, Inc., 1965), pp. 78-79.

37   Salaries. *Business Week,* May 15, 1965, pp. 90-118.

38   Pew, *New York Times,* June 28, 1965.

40   Watson, pp. 92-93.

47   General Motors, S.R. 1387, 85th Congress, 2nd Session.

50   Rise of new elites, see Daniel Bell, "The Post-Industrial
Society," Liberty Mutual Insurance Company Forum,
Boston, June 14th, 1962.

51   Military-industrial-political. See Duscha, cited above.

51   Research and development expenditures. Seymour Mel-
man. *Our Depleted Society* (New York: Holt, Rinehart
and Winston, 1965), p. 77.

52   One-third of the labor force. Eli Ginzberg, *The Plural-
istic Economy* (New York: McGraw-Hill Book Company, 1965), p. 144.

72   Top 2 percent. R. Lampman, National Bureau of Economic Research, *Occasional Paper #71,* p. 31.

PAGE 73 John Stuart Mill, *Principles of Political Economy*, Book II, Chap. 1.

74 *Privata lex.* I am indebted to Mr. Frederick Stern for this point.

77 Median earnings. *U. S. Statistical Abstract*, 1965, pp. 231-233; Workers aged 35-44, Mollie Orshanksy, "Consumption, Work and Poverty," in B. Seligman, *Poverty as a Public Issue* (New York: The Free Press of Glencoe, 1965), p. 80.

80 7.5 million individuals. Orshanksy, "Consumption," p. 69.

81 $11.5 billion. Orshanksy, p. 69.

81 Walinsky. *New Republic*, July 4, 1964, p. 15.

85 Concentration of Stock. R. Lampman, *Occasional Paper #71*, p. 26.

85-86 Tax Evasion. Philip Stern, *The Great Treasury Raid* (New York: Random House, Inc., 1964).

86 Chase Manhattan Bank, *Business in Brief*, January-February, 1960.

87 Income receivers in $15,000 and up bracket. *Survey of Current Business* (Department of Commerce, April, 1964), pp. 5-11.

93 Andrew Shonfield, *Modern Capitalism* (New York: Oxford University Press, 1965), p. 339.

95 "Economic men." Cf. A. Lowe, *On Economic Knowledge* (New York: Harper & Row, Publishers, 1965), Parts I and II.

99 Kappel, *Vitality*, p. 102.

104-105 Military-industrial complex. Duscha, *Arms*, pp. 63-64.

106 Victor Perlo, *Militarism and Industry* (New York: International Publishers Company, Inc., 1963), p. 124.

113 Costliness of clothes. W. Sombart, *The Quintessence of Capitalism* (New York: E. P. Dutton & Co., Inc., 1915), p. 123.

114 Kenneth Boulding, *The Meaning of the 20th Century* (New York: Harper & Row, 1964), p. 8.

PAGE 115 "Humbug." H. Neisser, *The Sociology of Knowledge* (New York: James Heineman, 1965), pp. 39-40. See also Don Price, *The Scientific Estate,* (Cambridge, Mass.: Harvard University Press, 1965), pp. 29-30; and A. R. J. P. Ubbelhode, "The Beginnings of the Change from Craft Mystery to Science as a Basis for Technology," in Singer, *et al.,* eds., *History of Technology* (New York: Oxford University Press, 1958), IV, p. 680.

128 A. J. Ayer. Daniel Bell, *Marxism-Leninism: A Doctrine on the Defensive* (New York: School of International Affairs, Columbia University, 1965), p. 15.

130 Alexis de Tocqueville, *The Old Regime* (Garden City, New York: Doubleday & Company, Inc. [Anchor Books], 1955), p. 86.

☆

INDEX

☆

143

☆

ACKNOWLEDGMENTS

☆

Although they are few in number, these pages have not been quick to write, and these essays have been through innumerable revisions over four years. During this process I have been much helped by the comments of a number of friends, including Daniel Bell, Samuel Coleman, Benjamin Kaplan, and Ben B. Seligman. I owe a special word of thanks to Theodore Draper for helping me find a proper frame for my thoughts and to Peter L. Bernstein for an especially searching critique. I am grateful as well to the University of Pennsylvania for the opportunity to deliver two lectures, "Capitalism and Technology" and "The Outlook for the Business System," that aided me greatly in formulating my ideas; to Earl Cheit of the University of California at Berkeley for giving me an opportunity to present a paper on the business ideology at a Ford Foundation workshop; to the *Scientific American* magazine for the chance to examine their data on managerial backgrounds; and to the *Atlantic Monthly* and *Commentary* for publishing, respectively, the first and second essays of the book, in somewhat shortened form. As always, however, my prime acknowledgment is to Adolph Lowe, my warmest critic and my severest supporter.

Let me thank as well Miss Jean Berman who typed an early version of the manuscript one lovely summer in Chilmark, and Miss Violet Serwin who typed a later one in New York City that fall.

ROBERT L. HEILBRONER

March, 1966